Cambridge Opera Handbooks

W. A. Mozart
Don Giovanni

W. A. Mozart
Don Giovanni

JULIAN RUSHTON

CAMBRIDGE UNIVERSITY PRESS

Cambridge
London   New York   New Rochelle
Melbourne   Sydney

Published by the Press Syndicate of the University of Cambridge
The Pitt Building, Trumpington Street, Cambridge CB2 1RP
32 East 57th Street, New York, NY 10022, USA
296 Beaconsfield Parade, Middle Park, Melbourne 3206, Australia

First published 1981

Printed in Great Britain
at the University Press, Cambridge

British Library Cataloguing in Publication Data

Rushton, Julian
W. A. Mozart, Don Giovanni – (Cambridge opera handbooks).
1. Mozart, Wolfgang Amadeus. Don Giovanni
I. Title   II. Series
782.1'092'4   ML410.M9   80-41534

ISBN 0 521 22826 3 hard covers
ISBN 0 521 29663 3 paperback

CAMBRIDGE OPERA HANDBOOKS

General preface

This is a series of studies of individual operas, written for the serious opera-goer or record-collector as well as the student or scholar. Each volume has three main concerns. The first is historical: to describe the genesis of the work, its sources or its relation to literary prototypes, the collaboration between librettist and composer, and the first performance and subsequent stage history. This history is itself a record of changing attitudes towards the work, and an index of general changes of taste. The second is analytical and is grounded in a very full synopsis which considers the opera as a structure of musical and dramatic effects. In most volumes there is also a musical analysis of a section of the score, showing how the music serves or makes the drama. The analysis, like the history, naturally raises questions of interpretation, and the third concern of each volume is to show how critical writing about an opera, like production and performance, can direct or distort appreciation of its structural elements. Some conflict of interpretation is an inevitable part of this account; editors of the handbooks reflect this — by citing classic statements, by commissioning new essays, by taking up their own critical position. A final section gives a select bibliography, a discography and guides to other sources.

In working out plans for these volumes, the Cambridge University Press was responding to an initial stimulus from staff of the English National Opera. Particular thanks are due to Mr Edmund Tracey and Mr Nicholas John for help, advice and suggestions.

Books published

Richard Wagner: *Parsifal* by Lucy Beckett
C.W. von Gluck: *Orfeo* by Patricia Howard

other volumes in preparation

In memory of my father
who, like Leopold Mozart, died while his son was at
work on *Don Giovanni*. I shall always be indebted to
the example of his knowledge and love of Mozart, and
of this work in particular.

Contents

Illustrations

Acknowledgments

I should like particularly to thank the other contributors to this volume,
Dr Edward Forman of the University of Bristol, whose essay (Chapter
3) is noteworthy for demonstrating da Ponte's indebtedness to the
popular tradition, and Bernard Williams, Provost of King's College,
Cambridge, whose magnificent summary of conceptions of Giovanni
has spared me a good deal of reading and is itself a highly original
contribution to the debate. I would also like to thank the discographer
of the series, Malcolm Walker; Michael Black, Clare Davies-Jones, Rose-
mary Dooley, and Ruth Smith of Cambridge University Press; for help
with illustrations, John Deathridge and David Charlton; for obtaining
copies of original libretti from the Gesellschaft der Musikfreunde in
Vienna, John Glofcheskie; for a lavish supply of reprints, Pierluigi
Petrobelli; and for discussion and ideas, the above-named, and also
Alexander Goehr, John Warrack, Edmund Tracey, Lionel Friend, Brian
Trowell, and Peter Branscombe. Figs. 1-4 are reproduced courtesy of
the Deutsches Theatermuseum, Munich.

                                                      Julian Rushton

King's College, Cambridge
September 1980

1 Introduction

Unique individuals as they are, not one of Mozart's great operas is without precedent, and *Don Giovanni* has complex relationships with two of its immediate predecessors. One is *Le nozze di Figaro,* the first completed collaboration of Mozart and Lorenzo da Ponte, performed in Vienna on 1 May 1786. The other is the *Don Giovanni* of Giovanni Bertati, performed at the S. Moisè theatre in Venice on 5 February 1787 with music by Giuseppe Gazzaniga. Some forty years on and in a new world, da Ponte claimed to have chosen the Don Juan legend as material peculiarly suited to Mozart's many-sided genius. He forgot to mention the existence of a new libretto, emanating from Venice where he had spent much of his hot youth and where, although he was now *persona non grata,* he retained contacts; but it was doubtless not without influence upon his choice.

Even as the Gazzaniga opera was being performed in Venice, Mozart was being fêted in Prague where, only a few months after its modest success in Vienna, *Figaro* was all the rage. Mozart wrote to Gottfried von Jacquin on 15 January 1787 of his own rather sober behaviour at a party:

However, I was very delighted to look upon all these people leaping about in sheer delight to the music of my figaro, adapted for noisy contredances and waltzes [teutsche] ; – for here nothing is discussed but – figaro; nothing is played, blowed, sung or whistled but – figaro: no opera is succeeding but – figaro and eternally figaro; certainly a great honour for me.[1]

On this visit, Mozart launched his 'Prague' symphony K.504, and directed a performance of *Figaro* on 20 January. When he left Prague on 8 February he had been invited to compose a new opera for the autumn season. The impresario, Pasquale Bondini, would obviously want more of the ingredients which had endeared *Figaro* to the public: melodious arias, involved ensembles, colourful orchestration, brilliant finales. Da Ponte and Mozart must have seen the possibilities of the

1

Don Juan material for similar treatment, cheerfully accepting unoriginality of subject in such promising circumstances.

Work on *Don Giovanni* extended over about twelve months before the first Vienna performance in May 1788. After his return from Prague Mozart composed among other works the two great string quintets in C and G minor (K.515 and K.516), and he made a set of three by adapting his C minor wind serenade as a quintet (K.516b/406). From May 1787 dates the great piano-duet sonata K.521. On 28 May Leopold Mozart died in Salzburg; but, whereas his mother's death in Paris in 1778 had considerably disturbed his compositional rhythm, Mozart apparently took his father's death in his stride. Yet this father—son relationship was intense and uneasy; it is deeply ingrained in an earlier opera (*Idomeneo*), and it may be that the impact of this death tapped some dark force in Mozart's creativity which welled up in *Don Giovanni*. Mozart's next works, however, might be considered insulting to the dead. On 4 June he wrote a poem to his dead starling, and later that month he finished his 'musical joke', K.522. In August he wrote the elegant *Eine kleine Nachtmusik* and his last piano and violin sonata, K.526. These works seem quite detached from the opera whose composition they must have interrupted; and since no letters or other sources inform us about its progress, legend had it for a long time that the entire work was set down in Prague in three weeks or so before the première. However, a recently discovered letter of Mozart's to his brother-in-law, dated 29 September, indicates that he only began the three-day journey to Prague on 1 October. The date of the first performance was then expected to be 14 October; it was to coincide with the honeymoon visit to Prague of the Archduchess Maria Theresia and Prince Anton Clemens of Saxony. Even the Mozart of legend would hardly have left himself only ten days to compose and stage an opera. It was around this journey that Eduard Mörike constructed his charming fiction *Mozart auf der Reise nach Prag* (1855).

More prosaic evidence about the composition is to be found in the papers used in Mozart's autograph manuscript.[2] Most scholars assume that the 'Vienna' paper was used in that city, and the smaller 'Prague' paper indicates precisely what was composed after Mozart's journey; but of course 'Prague' paper might only have been resorted to after supplies brought from Vienna had been exhausted. Nevertheless the general picture is clear. Most of *Don Giovanni* was completed in Vienna and some was sent ahead to Prague. Opinions differ as to how much was set down in Prague; it certainly included much of the recitative, which Mozart would always leave until the principal numbers had been composed (and which therefore sometimes appears on spare pages of 'Vienna' paper). Such comic business as the recitative before the grave-yard duet, and the supper music in the second finale, evolved partly through on-the-spot improvisation, a speciality of the *buffo* personnel at Prague. The list of numbers certainly written in Prague is: Overture, No. 6 (Masetto's aria), No. 14 (duet), and the second finale. It seems that nothing was added in Prague which did not form part of the plan of the opera worked out in advance in Vienna.[3] Mozart may have been late in finishing, but the double postponement of the première was not his fault. He accounted for it in a letter to Jacquin written on three days not available for rehearsals:

[15 October] No doubt you think my opera is over by now – but – there you've missed the mark; for one thing the local troupe is not as clever as they are in Vienna at studying a piece like this in so little time. Secondly, when I arrived I found hardly any advance work and organi-zation, so it would have been quite impossible to give it on the 14th, i.e. yesterday. So yesterday they gave my figaro...*Don Giovanni* is now fixed for the 24th; – [21 October]It was fixed for the 24th, but one of the *donne* fell ill and it had to be put off again; – as the com-pany is so small, the impresario is in a continual flap, having to nurse his people as much as he can, in case some sudden illness should fling him into the plightiest of plights, not being able to mount any show at all! – so everything goes slow here because the singers (from laziness) won't rehearse on opera days, and the entrepreneur (from fright and flap) won't insist . . . [25 October] This is the eleventh day that I've been scribbling this letter . . . the opera will be performed for the first time this coming Monday, the 29th . . .

Of all the legends connected with *Don Giovanni*, the most enduring, perhaps because it may even be true, is that the Overture was not com-posed until the night before the performance, and that on 29 October it was sight-read with the ink still wet on the orchestral parts. Several authorities insist that it was the penultimate night, and that the famous achievement of the Prague orchestra took place at the final rehearsal. The question is hardly one which deserves to generate much heat. Mozart entered the opening of the Overture (inaccurately) in his cata-logue and dated it 28 October, the day before the performance, but this proves nothing.[4]

In Prague Mozart stayed at the inn 'Bei drei goldenen Löwen' but spent much time, and wrote some of the music, at the Villa Bertramka belonging to his friends the Duscheks (now a Mozart museum). Da Ponte arrived on 8 October and stayed at the inn 'Zum Platteis', where he could talk with Mozart through the windows without either having to leave his room. The last details of the libretto will have been settled then, in readiness for printing, and da Ponte supervised some rehearsals. However, like the royal couple, he had to leave Prague before the première. Mozart directed the first four performances; the opera was very well received, even if it never created such a furore as *Figaro*. Mozart left for Vienna on 13 November. On the fifteenth Gluck died, and on 7 December Mozart was appointed imperial *Kammermusikus* in his stead, at less than half the salary. However, 800 florins annually compares well with the fees for *Don Giovanni*: in Prague, 100 ducats (450 florins) and in Vienna, 225 florins (da Ponte received about half these sums). *Don Giovanni* represents far more work than Mozart was ever asked to do for his official appointment.

In the months following his Prague visit Mozart's output was not large. Apart from a handful of songs and dances, he composed in Prague an aria for his hostess Josepha Duschek ('Bella mia fiamma', K.528). In Vienna he composed three of his finest movements for solo piano – the allegro and andante K.533 which form a sonata in F with the rondo K.494, and the B minor adagio K.540 – and his penultimate piano concerto, K.537. At the end of April he composed two arias, a duet, and the necessary recitatives for the Vienna production of *Don Giovanni* (No. 10a, dated 24 April; No. 21a, dated 28 April; No. 21b, dated 30 April), thus finishing just a week before the first performance on 7 May. The work was prepared with great speed, and was mounted by special order of the Emperor Joseph II, the protector of da Ponte and, although he did not really like his music, of Mozart also. His orders were necessary to overcome intrigue, but he was away at the Turkish war and saw only the last performance of the year, which was also the last in Vienna in Mozart's lifetime, on 15 December. Da Ponte's description of these performances is quite inaccurate, since he implies that the Emperor saw an early performance, and that the new music was composed after an unsuccessful première. Almost certainly the only alterations made between May and December were cuts, and the second authentic version of *Don Giovanni*, therefore, was in existence at the end of April. By August Mozart had composed not only two trios and various keyboard works, but his last three symphonies as well.

Since 1788 the career of Mozart's *Don Giovanni* has been almost as notorious as that of its protagonist. It is the second opera (*Figaro* is the first) to have remained continuously in the repertory; but unlike its elder sibling *Don Giovanni* was frequently so distorted as to be barely recognizable. Even today, when Mozart's other mature operas suffer no worse indignity than the omission of a few dramatically superfluous arias, *Don Giovanni* is regularly performed and recorded in an inauthentic form, an amalgam of the Prague and Vienna versions which tries to include everything except No. 21a and a few recitatives (see below, Chapter 4, 'The two authentic versions'). Critical exegesis of *Don Giovanni* is as plentiful as, and even more diverse than, that of *Die Zauberflöte*, and even the latter scarcely presents greater problems of staging and interpretation.[5] My debt to recent scholarly work will be apparent throughout, particularly to the edition of *Don Giovanni* by Wolfgang Plath and Wolfgang Rehm for the Neue Mozart Ausgabe, and to Christoph Bitter's *Wandlungen in den Inszenierungsformen des 'Don Giovanni'*; the work of the late Alfred Einstein is also of crucial importance to the student of this opera (see Select Bibliography). It is scarcely possible in a book of this size to do justice to the literature and performing history, which, indeed, are sometimes interwoven, for the influence of literature on stage interpretation goes back at least as far as E. T. A. Hoffmann. Unfortunately it was impossible to include a separate essay on the problems of staging *Don Giovanni*, but they are frequently touched on in the course of the book. One of the most sensitive of modern Mozart producers, Sir Peter Hall, is studied at work on the 1977 Glyndebourne production in John Higgins' *The Making of an Opera. Don Giovanni* has also been made into a film by Joseph Losey.

One question may be dealt with briefly here. There is no reason to suppose that any ambiguity of plot, genre, or meaning was intended by the authors, and the designation *dramma giocoso* applied to *Don Giovanni* by da Ponte cannot be used as evidence of any such intention. By this date it probably meant no more than the commoner term *opera buffa*. Da Ponte applied it also to *Così*, but Mozart entered both works as *opera buffa* in his personal catalogue. Da Ponte's American physician, Dr Francis, reported that 'Mozart determined to cast the opera exclusively as serious, and had well advanced in the work. Da Ponte assured me that he remonstrated and urged the expediency on the great composer of the introduction of the *vis comica*, in order to accomplish a greater success, and prepared the role with "Batti, batti", "Là ci darem", etc.'[6] Since prior versions of the subject used by da Ponte all include characters like Zerlina, and in view of the probable nature of the commission, for a successor to *Figaro*, this seems a most unlikely story. Nevertheless it would be bigoted to deny that *Don Giovanni* contains serious, even tragic, elements. It has been pointed out that *dramma giocoso* was originally used, at least by Goldoni, to mean an *opera buffa* which combined serious roles with comic (*parti serie* with *parti buffe*);

the *parti serie* did not compete with the *buffe* in ensembles and finales (whereas in Mozart they do).[7] There was also an intermediate type, *parti di mezzo carattere*, ranging from seriousness to farce. Some years earlier Mozart had conceived the idea of an *opera buffa* with these three kinds of role. He writes to his father that he has read through a hundred libretti without finding anything suitable. There is a promising poet in Vienna called da Ponte, but he seems to be in league with Salieri; in desperation, he thinks of Varesco, the Salzburg abbé who wrote *Idomeneo*; will Leopold impress on him that 'the most important thing is that as a whole it must be really comic and if possible should have 2 equally good *female roles* (frauenzimmer Rollen) − one must be Seria, but the other *Mezzo Carattere* − but in quality − both roles must be quite equal. − The third female role, however, can be quite Buffa, and so if necessary can all the men' (7 May 1783). Anna, Elvira, and Zerlina fill these categories far more exactly than the women in any other Mozart opera, although one of the men, Ottavio, is also predominantly a *seria* role.

Whether or not we believe, as Mozart did, that in opera music is supreme and the poetry but its 'obedient daughter', the study of an opera must start with the libretto. Most 'problems' of *Don Giovanni* arise there, since it is not a closely knit intrigue like *Figaro* or *Così* but an ingenious compilation from literary, popular, and musical predecessors. Unfortunately we know nothing about Mozart's personal involvement in its construction. Da Ponte is as silent on this as on his debt to Bertati. Doubtless Mozart was closely involved, as we know him to have been on other occasions. There is a tendency to credit him with any good ideas, but to blame da Ponte for the defects that remain. The critics cannot have it both ways, and if the libretto is defective, Mozart must either take some of the blame or be assumed not to have bothered himself with it − which would be blameworthy indeed. Nevertheless it is emphatically not da Ponte's choice and treatment of the subject which have provoked the commentators, men of letters, and philosophers, but the music. It is not Tirso, nor Molière, not Goldoni, nor da Ponte, who arouse such interest in the personalities involved that studies of some of them have attained the proportions of a short biography. It is Mozart; and his, too, is the responsibility for the seriousness with which we take many of the situations, and for the demonic element so often detected in *Don Giovanni*, which is something quite different from the pantomime devilry so often associated with the subject. Mozart is thus the catalyst whose influence changed the subject from the proper interest of Latin Europe and Catholic morality, and from the status of both vulgar and enlightened entertainment, to the proper interest of Northern, Faustian philosophy. With *Die Zauberflöte* no serious commentator could fail to conclude that the comedy is a cheerful enhancement of a fundamentally serious work. With *Don Giovanni* the issue is by no means so clear, and therein lies much of its fascination. Its influence on literature and philosophy is unmatched by any opera before Wagner; yet, at bottom, it is not the embodiment of a philosophy, nor a moral tract, but an *opera buffa*.

2 Synopsis

Scarcely any published synopsis of *Il dissoluto punito o sia Il Don Giovanni* is altogether free of errors or unwarrantable glosses. I can hardly hope to succeed where so many have failed, but the following is presented with the simple aim of accurately representing the action as da Ponte and Mozart seem to have intended it. If the reader finds unexpected details or lacunae, it may be because he is accustomed to the accretions of nearly two centuries of mistranslation and a 'tradition' of interpretation which departed very rapidly from the atmosphere in which *Don Giovanni* was created (see below, pp. 68 ff). Problems of timing and action, including some well-established traditions which are not necessarily wrong but which should be recognized as lacking authority, are discussed in Chapter 4. The principal sources for a synopsis must be the very rare authentic libretti published for the Prague (1787) and Vienna (1788) performances, the preliminary libretto of 1787 (see below, Chapter 1, n. 3), and the text as it appears in Mozart's autograph. The Neue Mozart Ausgabe score distinguishes typographically between stage-directions from different sources. Such directions are particularly full in the Prague libretto, and several are traditionally omitted; they are incorporated or paraphrased here, since their authority is undoubted. Where the Prague and Vienna versions diverge, they are given in parallel columns. In scene-headings, material in square brackets is editorial; unattributed commentary in round brackets and in inverted commas is Leporello's, except in No. 10 (Act I Scene 13), where Ottavio is speaking.

Dramatis personae

Don Giovanni	A young and extremely licentious nobleman	Baritone
Donna Anna	A lady, betrothed to'	Soprano
Don Ottavio		Tenor
The Commendatore	[Father to Donna Anna]	Bass

8

Donna Elvira	A lady from Burgos, abandoned by Don Giovanni	Soprano
Leporello	Don Giovanni's servant	Bass
Masetto	[Peasant] in love with	Bass
Zerlina	Country girl	Soprano

Chorus of peasants and girls; servants; subterranean chorus
Stage instrumentalists
The action takes place in a city in Spain

Act I

Overture (Andante – allegro)

This is Mozart's closest approach to Gluck's practice of involving the overture with the action. It opens with the music for the stone guest (Act II, No. 24.5), modified in details: because there are no voices, the orchestral articulation is more precise, and the trombones are withheld for the actual apparition. This andante may well strike awe in the hearer, and so reverberate in his mind to prepare for the inevitable termination of Giovanni's adventures. It was the first time Mozart had used a slow introduction for an overture; he was to do so again in *Così* and *Die Zauberflöte*. The allegro begins with the bustling accompaniment and sprightly fanfare which are the normal stuff of overtures. The main theme, with its partly chromatic upward thrust, is so original that it has often been taken to portray the protagonist. It does not appear in the opera, so this interpretation cannot be confirmed; but the electrifying rhythms and swift transitions of mood make such an interpretation of the whole allegro very plausible. Other glosses, for example 'explaining' the prominent five-note falling motif introduced in the dominant as Justice in pursuit of the rascal, are merely fanciful, and are reminiscent of the nineteenth-century habit of composing programmatic overtures, a procedure which there is no likelihood of Mozart's having contemplated; the adventurous development of this figure could just as well be regarded as lively play, and thus as eminently Giovanni-esque. The allegro is a fully-fledged sonata form (whereas in *Figaro* Mozart had dispensed with a central development). For coda, however, Mozart devised a transition which leads directly into the first scene; it is a late development of the five-note figure, and the harmony takes us from D major towards the F major of 'Notte e giorno faticar'. There exists an authentic ending in D major, only two bars longer; its purpose is unclear. Longer, spurious concert-endings are still sometimes heard.

First tableau

[Half stage]   Night, a garden [possibly enclosed; belonging to the Commendatore's house].

Scene 1 No. 1 INTRODUCTION (Molto allegro. Leporello: 'Notte e giorno faticar'). Leporello, cloaked, is on sentry duty, whiling away the time with his eternal complaint: he must watch night and day while his master takes his pleasure. Why cannot *he* play the gentleman? He hears someone coming and hides. Giovanni enters pursued by Anna, who is holding on to him and trying to uncover his face. He angrily tries to shake her off, calling her crazy and saying that she will never learn who he is. Leporello cowers; but his anxiety comes close to dominating the trio, preserving the *opera buffa* tone which he has already established. Anna hears her father coming; she releases her attacker and goes indoors. The Commendatore accosts Giovanni and forces him to fight, but is quickly overcome by his agile opponent. In a short trio (andante) the Commendatore gasps out his life, Leporello stands horrified, and Giovanni, who had at first refused to fight such an unequal battle, himself seems shocked, even a little moved. **Scene 2** (Recitative). Giovanni calls Leporello, who asks 'Are you dead, or is it the old man?' and coarsely applauds: 'Bravo! two fine deeds, seducing the daughter and killing the father.' He is nearly beaten for his impertinence – Giovanni recovers easily from shock – and they slip away. **Scene 3** Ottavio, Anna, and servants enter with lights. To the dry practicality of their search succeeds a searing orchestral dissonance as Anna sees the body. **No. 2 DUET** (Recitativo obbligato. Anna: 'Ma qual mai s'offre, oh Dei, spettacolo funesto agli occhi miei!'). She falls on the body, finding blood, but no breath; its limbs are cold. She faints. Ottavio, anxious but practical, calls for assistance (smelling-salts, spirits), and orders the body to be removed. With characteristic impetuosity he is already saying 'Console yourself. . .take heart', and this, with the invitation to marry him which, in effect, follows, will be his refrain throughout the opera. Anna revives (Allegro. Anna: 'Fuggi, crudele'). She seems to reject Ottavio, but possibly mistakes him for her father's murderer: 'Fly, cruel man, and let me die too, now that he who gave me life is dead.' Ottavio brings her to her senses, and she begs his forgiveness, and asks for her father. His reply ('You have both husband and father in me') is eloquent, although possibly a little out of place at such a moment; her response is a demand for vengeance. He swears by her eyes and by their love, and the scene ends sombrely with their voices united in some awe at this oath.

Second tableau

[Full stage] Night, but near dawn [the following morning]. A street. [An inn, at which Elvira is staying; a glimpse of Giovanni's house.]

Scene 4 (Recitative). Leporello asks permission to be frank; he deplores his master's way of life. Giovanni brushes the familiar criticism aside and begins to tell of a new adventure he has in mind. Suddenly he smells a woman (Leporello is forced into admiration). **Scene 5** Elvira enters in travelling clothes. **No. 3 ARIA** (with the men's voices added: 'Ah chi mi dice mai, quel barbaro dov'è'). Every other aria in *Don Giovanni*, with the exception of the two added for Vienna in 1788, is addressed to someone on the stage. This one is a soliloquy; but through operatic convéntion it is sung, and being sung it can be overheard. Elvira's public proclamation of her afflictions may appear a little eccentric, especially in view of their equivocal nature. But she sings with dignity and spirit, asking where she will find her betrayer and rehearsing his punishment. All unknowing, Giovanni is unctuously sympathetic and prepares to console her ('As he's consoled eighteen hundred others'). The music closes, but poised above the cadence is Giovanni's courteous approach: 'Signorina'. (Recitative). She turns; recognition is immediate. While Giovanni recoils she calls him names ('She certainly knows him well') and indicts him for seducing her in her home, promising marriage, then deserting her ('she talks just like a book'). Giovanni says that if she will not believe him when he tells her how urgent were his reasons for departure, surely she will believe his honest servant; and while her back is turned he escapes. Leporello assures her that he is not worth pursuit. She is neither the first nor the last, as she can see by reading the catalogue of conquests which he has drawn up. **No. 4 ARIA** (Allegro — andante con moto. 'Madamina, il catalogo è questo'). With joy he enumerates; 640 in Italy, 231 in Germany, 100 in France, 91 in Turkey, but in Spain, ah, in Spain, 1003 *so far*. He waxes lyrical about the diversity of womankind: the blond, the brown, the plump, the slender, the tall, the short, and, particularly, the young and untried. He ends with the grossest innuendo: 'just so long as they wear a skirt, you know what will happen'. He leaves. **Scene 6** (Recitative). Elvira, contemplating revenge, goes in. **Scene 7** [During Scenes 4–5 day has broken; a short time-lapse may be understood, so that now it is full daylight and perhaps 10 a.m.] A festive party of peasants appears, dancing, playing instruments, and singing. **No. 5 CHORUS** (led by Zerlina and Masetto: 'Giovinette che fate all'amore'). **Scene 8** Giovanni and Leporello come on the scene and the gallant patronizes the company, offering to 'take the bride under his protection' (a scuffle in the crowd; Leporello is also trying to take someone under his protection). Giovanni invites everyone to feast at his house; Leporello is to lead the way, leaving Zerlina with him. Masetto objects; his bride cannot remain without him. She seems all too content to remain 'in the hands of a cavalier'; and Masetto, who knows very well what those hands might do, is only subdued by a flash of the gentleman's sword. Nevertheless he has his say. **No. 6 ARIA** ('Ho capito, signor, si'). 'I understand; you are the gentleman and do as you please. (To Leporello) I'm coming! (To Zerlina) All right, you bitch, stay, and see if he makes you a lady.' **Scene 9** Giovanni quickly overcomes Zerlina's protestations of duty and doubts as to his sincerity; she is too good for such a bumpkin, and he will marry her himself. There follows the most perfect duet of seduction imaginable. **No. 7 DUET** ('Là ci darem la mano'). Her continued resistance is merely verbal; she accepts his melody, intoxicated by this apparition of a noble lover, and yields most sweetly ('Andiam mio bene', change of metre without change of speed). **Scene 10** (Recitative). As they move off, arm in arm, towards Giovanni's mansion, Elvira pounces, denouncing the seducer. Aside, he protests to her that he is only amusing himself; but she cries aloud that she knows what *that* means. He tells Zerlina that this is a poor mad thing in love with him, whom he must humour, but Elvira turns to the girl with an awful warning. **No. 8 ARIA** ('Ah, fuggi il traditor'). She whisks Zerlina away. **Scene 11** (Recitative). Giovanni is so taken aback by the moral energy of Elvira (doubtless supported by jealousy) that he is uncharacteristically reduced to grumbling: 'Ma par ch'oggi il demonio si diverta d'opporsi a miei piacevoli progressi; vanno mal tutti quanti.' 'It seems that today the devil is amusing himself by obstructing the path of my pleasures; everything is going wrong.' Worse is to come, for Anna and Ottavio enter, in search of assistance in tracing the unknown assailant. They address Giovanni as one well known to them, and as a gallant man who will help them; he is relieved at this unsuspecting approach, and, considering that he should not know what is wrong, he almost overdoes his offer of support: 'Questa man, questo ferro, i beni, il sangue spenderò per servirvi . . .' 'This hand, this sword, my wealth, my blood, I will expend to serve you . . .'). **Scene 12** Before they can reply Elvira bursts in once more. Having accosted Giovanni ('Ah, at it again, monster of iniquity') she turns with a quite altered tone to Anna. **No. 9 QUARTET** (Elvira: 'Non ti fidar, o misera, di quel ribaldo cor'). She urges Anna to place no confidence in such a villain. Anna and Ottavio are startled, but at once perceive Elvira's noble bearing; the marks of suffering fill them with pity. Giovanni, baffled once more, falls back on the trick of persuading them that Elvira is mad; he can calm her if they are left alone. She overhears and denounces him, taking off into heady flights of coloratura as the others try to master the situation. Ottavio does not know what to think, Anna remarks that Elvira does not look mad, Giovanni and Elvira exchange abuse ('Madwoman!' 'Liar!'). Giovanni hisses that she should not be so imprudent as to display her wrongs in public, in view of their nature, but she retorts that she has abandoned prudence, and evidently does not care if she seems ridiculous. At the end of the quartet she goes out. (Recitative). Giovanni says he will follow her and see that she comes to no harm; then he excuses himself to Anna and invites her, all too pressingly, to come to his house if she requires assistance. **Scene 13 No. 10** (Recitativo obbligato. Anna: 'Don Ottavio, son morta!'). Elvira's second interruption has so unbalanced Giovanni that he overplays his protestations of friendship; the tone of his last words has irresistibly recalled the man who invaded her room the previous night. We are again in the dramatic atmosphere of the third scene, even of *opera seria*, as she calls on the gods to witness that this was her father's murderer. Despite her explanation (Recitativo secco) Ottavio is understandably incredulous; the man was a friend, and, as he remarks when left alone, a cavalier. Anna formally narrates her experience (Recitativo obbligato; 'Era già alquanto avanzata la notte'). The orchestra begins with sustained chords which progressively fragment; at the climax, when she remembers having screamed, it returns to the urgent, disjointed motif of the beginning. It was already late; she was alone 'by mischance' when a cloaked man entered whom at first she took for Ottavio. She soon saw her mistake from his behaviour as he approached. He embraced her; she cried out and no one came. He stifled her cries; 'I thought myself vanquished' ('The villain! go on!'). My force returned, she says, and by turning and twisting I broke free of him ('Oof! I breathe again!'). Now she screamed so loudly that the man fled; she followed him to the street 'pursuing the pursuer'. Her father came, and the rest Ottavio knows. **ARIA** ('Or sai chi l'onore rapire à me volse'). Honour demands revenge; she recalls the bloody scene and urges Ottavio to action. **Scene 14** (Recitative). Ottavio, alone, seems only half convinced; it is his first task to establish the truth, so that he can undeceive Anna or avenge her.

Vienna 1788 version only
No. 10a. ARIA ('Dalla sua pace'). All his happiness depends on hers.

Scene 15 (Recitative). Leporello and Giovanni find each other. How goes it, asks the master? Badly, says the man; but he has evidently been doing Giovanni's dirty work rather well. The peasants were settling down to enjoy themselves, although Masetto was sullen, when Elvira turned up with Zerlina and, as Giovanni correctly guesses, 'said all the ill of me she could think of'. Leporello, however, has contrived to lock her out of the house. This last news puts Giovanni into excellent spirits. What was so well begun, he knows well how to finish, and he looks forward to entertaining the sweet country girls till nightfall. **No. 11 ARIA** ('Fin ch'an dal vino'). Leporello is instructed to let the wine flow freely and bring in all the girls he can find. Let the dances be all mixed up; for some the minuet, for some the folia, for some the allemanda, and tomorrow there will be another ten names on the list.

Third tableau

[Half stage] Garden [of Giovanni's mansion, overlooked by its windows], with two doors locked from the outside and two niches. [Midday, or at latest, early afternoon.]

Scene 16 Masetto, Zerlina, and peasants scattered about, sitting or sleeping on the grass. (Recitative). Masetto is sullen and accusing; Zerlina tries to convince him that nothing happened between her and the cavalier, and uses all her art to win him over. **No. 12 ARIA** (with 'cello obbligato: 'Batti, batti, o bel Masetto'). He can beat her or pluck out her eyes, if only they are friends afterwards. (Recitative). Masetto is bewitched, as well he might be. But Giovanni's voice is heard within; Zerlina is frightened and confused, and Masetto's suspicions instantly revive. At this point the first finale begins. **No. 13 FINALE No. 13.1** (Allegro assai. Masetto: 'Presto, presto, pria ch'ei venga'). Masetto decides to spy, hidden in a niche, and Zerlina's attempt to dissuade him only increases his jealous rage. **Scene 17** Giovanni enters with four servants. There is no change of tempo or key, but the music suddenly becomes festive, with trumpets and drums. He invites the company into the house; the servants echo him in a brief chorus, and the stage is cleared but for Giovanni and Zerlina. **Scene 18 No. 13.2** (Andante). The music is hushed, voluptuous. Zerlina makes futile efforts to hide, but it sounds as if the magnetism of Giovanni has momentarily caused her to forget the danger to Masetto. Giovanni tries to resume where 'Là ci darem' broke off; he draws her towards the niche in which Masetto is hiding. The cavalier is momentarily confused, but yields Zerlina to Masetto in an ironic exchange. Sounds are heard from the ballroom. No. 13.3 (on-stage orchestra, the Contredanse). The three go in together. **Scene 19** Ottavio, intent on detection, enters with Anna and Elvira; all three are masked (no change of tempo, but a complete change of mood with the significant key-change from F major to D minor). Elvira seems to be the leader of the scheme to spy on Giovanni; she urges courage and prudence and Ottavio supports her. Anna, clearly nervous, thinks of the danger to them all, but to Ottavio in particular. Leporello opens a window, and the cadence of the Minuet floats out. **No. 13.4** (on-stage orchestra, Minuet). Leporello points out the maskers to Giovanni and at his behest asks them in. Ottavio accepts with grave formality. Leporello remarks that 'My friend [*sic*] can try to make love to these as well', an unconscious irony in view of what they have already experienced from Giovanni. **No. 13.5** (Adagio). The three together commend their enterprise to Heaven, in a ravishing movement in which the voices are supported only by wind instruments, a moment of eternity before the swirl of the dance and the rapid action to come.

Fourth tableau

[Full stage] Interior, lit up and ready for feasting the dancing. [The first interior set; the use of three dance orchestras suggests a three-part division of the set as if into three adjoining rooms. Giovanni has asked for confusion in No. 11: 'Senza alcun ordine la danza sia.' But unless the dances were separated it is difficult to see how the device of having Masetto dance a different step could be expected to prevent the attempted abduction of Zerlina from being observed.] **Scene 20 No. 13.6** (Allegro, the music unmistakably like No. 5). A dance has just finished. Giovanni and Leporello invite the company to rest, and they call for refreshments. Masetto cautions Zerlina; they agree that so much sweetness could end bitterly. Giovanni begins to flirt with her (and Leporello with some other girls). Zerlina clearly enjoys it and she dislikes Masetto's very obvious jealousy. **No. 13.7** (Maestoso, an abrupt change of key bringing the return of the festive trumpets and drums). The three maskers enter; formally greeted, they give thanks and join Giovanni and Leporello in the refrain 'Viva la libertà', a phrase susceptible of various interpretations. For Giovanni it may well imply licence; for the respectable trio, simply Liberty Hall, an acknowledgement that they are welcome to preserve their incognito; for the audience, versed in the political implications left between the lines of *Le nozze di Figaro,* it might have meant political liberty, an interpretation supported by the otherwise disproportionately vigorous setting Mozart gives it.[1] Giovanni orders more dancing. **No. 13.8 DANCE SCENE** (Minuet, Contredanse, Allemanda, called 'Teitsch' for 'Deutsche Tänze'; played by three on-stage groups). Ottavio leads Anna to dance the aristocratic **Minuet**, although she is nearly fainting. Elvira points out the intended victim. The confusion is preparing; 'Va bene', remarks Giovanni, and is ironically echoed by the watchful Masetto. The Minuet is played by a small string orchestra with oboes and horns; the second group, consisting of a violin and double bass, is heard tuning. Leporello is ordered to busy himself with Masetto, and Giovanni approaches Zerlina. The **Contredanse** is played by the second group and danced by Giovanni and Zerlina; a dance neither aristocratic nor merely bucolic, but the middle ground on which these two meet. The third group, constituted like the second, is heard tuning. Ottavio and Elvira are occupied with supporting Anna. Leporello bullies Masetto into dancing, and they begin the **Teitsch** (third group). At this point there are three simultaneous dance-metres, the governing $\frac{3}{4}$ (Minuet), $\frac{2}{4}$ (Contredanse, three bars to two of the Minuet), and $\frac{3}{8}$ (Teitsch, three bars to one of the Minuet). Each person dancing adheres to the metre of the dance when singing, so that Zerlina's cry 'O numi, son tradita' fits with the Contredanse but not the Minuet, Masetto's agitated cries adopt the faster notes of the Teitsch, and the maskers sing resolutely with the Minuet. The music is not loud, so that every word can be heard, and, in order to fit the dances together, Mozart had to eschew any but the simplest harmony. Nevertheless by this combination of metres (which is incidentally the only passage in *Don Giovanni* for which a sketch survives) he works up an almost unbearable tension. The stage-directions here are so full, particularly in the Prague libretto, and are so often misunderstood, that they are given in full below (p. 61). Zerlina is drawn, resisting, out of the room. Masetto perceives it, breaks free of Leporello, and runs out in pursuit. Leporello, muttering 'Here's a disaster brewing', hastens out as well, and the maskers rather complacently remark that the enemy is bringing about his own downfall. Then Zerlina screams; sounds of struggle are heard. The dances stop abruptly and the musicians and peasants melt away, leaving the stage clear for the principals. **No. 13.9** (Allegro assai. Zerlina: 'Gente, aiuto'). The three on stage run to help; Masetto is heard calling off-stage; a new scream, and struggling, come from the other side. The doors have been locked, but Ottavio and the others break one down just as Zerlina bursts in from another direction, still crying out (see below, Chapter 4, n. 24). **No. 13.10** (Andante maestoso). Leporello has small thanks for his timely warning; Giovanni drags him on, sword in hand, shamelessly accusing him of the attack. It is doubtful if such a story would have deceived even the peasants whom he must be expecting to encounter. Ottavio, pistol in hand, gives him the lie; he and the ladies unmask in turn. Giovanni is confounded, and when all call him traitor, and Zerlina leads them in saying that everyone now knows of his villainy ('Tutto, tutto già si sà'), he makes no reply. No. 13.11 (Allegro. 'Trema, trema, o scellerato'). The five together invoke the thunder of revenge. At first Giovanni feels really threatened (so does Leporello; they sing the same music). In a sudden hush, Giovanni is heard to declare that his courage remains unshaken (he has a new melodic idea; Leporello can now only echo the words in his own patter: 'his courage is unshaken'). Thus the act ends (*più stretto*) with the five in chorus declaring that retribution will visit him that very day, and Giovanni, backed by Leporello, declaring that he fears nothing.

Act II

First tableau

[Full stage] A street. [Elvira's lodging, with balcony; early evening, and not yet dark.]

Scene 1 No. 14 DUET (Giovanni 'Eh via buffone, non mi seccar'). In a brilliant *buffo* duet Giovanni mocks Leporello who, however, seems almost serious in his intention to quit: the master has gone too far. (Recitative). Giovanni calls him back as he makes to go and finds the necessary argument, money. Leporello tries to exact a promise to leave playing with women; Giovanni replies with amused astonishment: 'Lasciar le donne! Pazzo! sai ch'elle per me son necessarie più del pan che mangio, più dell'aria che spiro!' 'Leave women! Idiot! don't you know that they are more necessary to me than the bread I eat, than the air I breathe!' Leporello asks how he has the heart to deceive them all: 'E tutto amore. Chi a una sola è fedele, verso l'altre è crudele.' 'It is all love; to be faithful to one is to be cruel to the rest.' Leporello, easily impressed by speeches, seems prepared to fall in with the next plan, the seduction of Elvira's maid; he puts up a token resistance to exchanging clothes with his master, but they swap cloaks and hats as darkness begins to fall.
Scene 2 No. 15 TRIO (Elvira: 'Ah, taci, ingiusto core'. The comedy of disguise is intended to get rid of Elvira; Giovanni therefore sings from behind Leporello.) First, she proclaims her tangled thoughts; the events

of the day, the quiet of the evening, lead her to feel pity for her be-trayer. Giovanni seizes his advantage; Leporello murmurs that she is mad to listen. Having won her attention Giovanni, with an eloquent key-change, tries the ploy of a serenade, using the melody of No. 16 and a similar *galant* sentiment: 'Discendi, o gioja bella': 'Come down, my fair delight, you shall see that you are the one my whole soul adores, already I am penitent.' Angrily, and with angular phrases, she expresses disbelief; he responds with growing urgency, threatening suicide, at which Leporello is afraid of bursting with laughter. The voices come to-gether; it is accomplished. Time stands still as Elvira reproaches herself with weakness, Leporello expresses sympathy for her, and Giovanni compliments himself on his skill. She goes in. (Recitative). While she comes down Leporello is forced to agree to take her off (the Prague lib-retto indicates that he is persuaded by a flash of a pistol, but it is suffi-cient for Giovanni to make a little show of violence). Giovanni stands aside. **Scene 3** After a nervous start Leporello warms to his role and Elvira seems convinced by his protestations of fidelity. Giovanni shouts out as if killing somebody; they run away and he comes forward laugh-ing. He then sings his serenade. **No. 16 CANZONETTA** (mandoline ob-bligato, the instrument held by the singer: 'Deh vieni alla finestra'). The song is in two verses and its delectable melody has been traced in a col-lection ostensibly of folk-song, although it might also have originated in the middle of the trio No. 15.[2] **Scene 4** (Recitative). Giovanni sees someone at the window: 'that'll be her. . . psst!' But it is not his day. Masetto is heard approaching with his scarecrow army, armed with swords, arquebus, pistols. Giovanni quickly sizes up the situation and plays the role of a servant willing to betray his odious master. **No. 17 ARIA** ('Metà di voi qua vadano'). In this witty *parlando* aria, the very opposite of the lyrical manner of the Canzonetta, Giovanni directs the peasants: half of you go this way, half go that, and when you see a man with a girl, attack him. Maliciously, he describes the white-plumed hat, the cloak and sword, now worn by Leporello. He hustles the peasants off, keeping Masetto with him. **Scene 5** (Recitative). By plausible talk he relieves Masetto of his armoury, beats him soundly with the flat of his sword, and goes his way; he is not seen again until the graveyard scene. **Scene 6** Zerlina, with a light, comes upon the groaning Masetto. She is in a mood to attach herself to him; she remarks what trouble his jealousy has caused but quickly sets about comforting him, which she does as lusciously as possible. **No. 18 ARIA** ('Vedrai, carino'). She has a very special remedy, which she indicates by allowing him to place his hand on her heart. They go off together to a gentle orchestral coda, fully reconciled; soon, however, they are in the hunt again.

Second tableau

[Half stage] A dark courtyard or porch with three doors [at Anna's house]. [It is now quite dark, at least on stage; all the darker, perhaps, for the brightness of the moon, noted by Giovanni in the graveyard shortly afterwards.]

Scene 7 (Recitative). Leporello is trying to give Elvira the slip. He comes into the enclosed court because he has seen lights in the road; she wonders what there is to be ashamed of. He leaves her in a dark corner to search for the way out. **No. 19 SEXTET** (Elvira: 'Sola, sola in bujo loco'). Elvira's last words in recitative — 'Ah, do not leave me' — give rise to her opening of the sextet — 'Alone in this dark place, I feel my heart thumping' — and Mozart, a past-master at the economical suggestion of feeling, begins with a nervous, ambiguous curve on the wind and a trembling figure in the violins. The sequel is one of his greatest ensembles, the andante in particular being masterly in its combination of diverse feelings within one musical tempo and continuity. From Elvira's opening melody, breathless but fully formed, and not used again, we turn to Leporello, with whom the string trills seem to grope in sympathy; then he finds a door: 'Now it's time to run away'. In two chords Mozart changes key (from B flat to D) and thus brings on the lights, borne by the servants of Anna and Ottavio. The light on stage glows in harmony with the soft entry of trumpets and drums. Leporello conceals himself and, oblivious of the uninvited company, Ottavio resumes his plea to Anna to calm herself; her father's ghost will suffer from her torment. Anna replies in a still more melting phrase which begins with an unmistakable, if fortuitous, allusion to No. 2 (the duet, 'Fuggi, crudele'). She insists that only death can end her mourning, and her voice surmounts the only rapid key-changes of the whole movement, apt symbol of her turbulent feelings. The music settles into C minor. Elvira is heard again, and the violins introduce a drooping chromatic figure which dominates much of the rest of this section. She is seeking for her 'Giovanni'; he (Leporello) mutters that it is all up if he is seen. Both spot the door and head for it from different directions, Leporello doubtless well in advance. **Scene 8** He reaches the door, to find his path blocked by Zerlina and Masetto. With Anna and Ottavio they quickly surround him and threaten to execute him on the spot. The drooping figure intervenes; Elvira steps forward to plead for the life of her 'husband' ('marito', not the vaguer 'sposo' which may only mean betrothed). There is general consternation; but the four recover and cry 'No! he must die! '; one can almost hear the swish of a sword between the anguished cries of Elvira. Ottavio is about to kill 'Giovanni' when he falls to his knees and reveals himself as Leporello, uttering an exaggeratedly lachrymose plea for mercy. The moment is both pathetic and funny; Leporello is really afraid, Elvira is deeply humiliated, and the others are stupefied. (Molto allegro). The sextet ends with an enormous finale in which all six begin with the same words, although Leporello is singled out, hoping for a miracle to save his skin. As for the others, they are quite bemused; it has been a terrible day. Anna, unable to take any more, goes off with the servants.

From this point until the graveyard scene the Prague and Vienna versions diverge; they are therefore presented here in parallel columns (see below, Chapter 4, 'The two authentic versions').

PRAGUE, 1787

Scene 9 (Recitative). The four upbraid Leporello, Elvira with deceit, the peasants with beating up Masetto. **No. 20 ARIA** ('Ah, pietà, Signori miei'). Running from one to another to apologize (Elvira), deny knowledge of the crime (Zerlina), and explain his trespass (Ottavio), Leporello contrives to reach the door and escape. **Scene 10** (Recitative). No one can stop him; Masetto says he has winged feet. Ottavio announces to all ('Amici miei', although two of his 'friends' are the peasants) that Giovanni is certainly the murderer of Anna's father; he will go to the authorities. **No. 21 ARIA** ('Il mio tesoro intanto'). In this beautiful and elaborate aria, the gentle Ottavio asks them to console his beloved and assure her that vengeance will not be long delayed. All leave the stage. [Scene 11 follows.]

VIENNA, 1788

Scene 9 (Recitative). The four upbraid Leporello, Elvira with deceit, the peasants with beating up Masetto. He stammers out that it is all his master's fault; he had tried to escape the lights, and ran in circles trying to hide. . . and in illustrating this he finds himself near the door and escapes. (The recitative, all with harpsichord accompaniment, ends with the escaping music from the omitted aria No. 20.) **Scene 10** The peasants run after him. Ottavio announces to Elvira that Giovanni is certainly the murderer of Anna's father; he will go to the authorities. They go their separate ways. **Scene 10a** Sarcastically singing the same phrase to which Leporello escaped, Zerlina arrives, dragging him by the hair, and preparing sadistic torments for him (she still believes him responsible for the

VIENNA, 1788

attack on Masetto). She ties him up, and calls for help; a peasant appears (mute role). **No. 21a DUET** (Leporello: 'Per queste tue manine'). He is bound to a chair, and the chair to a window-frame, flattering and pleading; but she shows no sign of relenting, evidently enjoys the fun, and only wishes she had his master at her mercy. **Scene 10b** (Recitative). Zerlina goes in search of Masetto, and Leporello gets rid of the peasant by the old trick of begging for a glass of water. He tugs the window-frame free from its hinges (helped by a plea to Mercury, the wing-footed patron of thieves) and escapes with all the clutter on his back. **Scene 10c** Zerlina returns with Elvira; they have had time only to register bafflement at the escape when Masetto arrives and explains his absence. By good luck he came upon a man molesting a girl; the man fled, but he is sure it was Giovanni. He and Zerlina go to inform Ottavio, who will act for them all. **Scene 10d No. 21b RECITATIVO OBBLIGATO and ARIA** ('In quali eccessi, o numi'; 'Mi tradì quell'alma ingrata'). Elvira reflects on this new outrage. She seems to see the chasm opening beneath Giovanni: 'Unhappy Elvira, what warring thoughts are born within you.' He has betrayed her; but she feels pity for him and no longer seeks for revenge. [Scene 11 follows.]

Third tableau

[Full stage] An enclosed place in the form of a cemetery. Various equestrian statues; statue of the Commendatore. [Moonlight. It is now about 10 p.m.; Leporello appears directly from his previous escape. It is not clear whether the Commendatore's statue is meant to be equestrian.]

Scene 11 (Recitative). Giovanni leaps over the wall, laughing. 'Now let her look for me'; clearly he is escaping from an indignant woman. 'What a night! brighter than day. It might be made for chasing girls. Is it late? Oh, it is not yet two hours into the night.' ('E tardi? Oh ancor non sono due della notte.') He wonders how Leporello is getting on, and on hearing his grumbling outside, calls him in. (They may exchange clothes, but this is explicit only in the Vienna version, with some new recitative.) Leporello gets no sympathy; was it not an honour to be nearly killed through being taken for his master? And Giovanni relates how he has been getting on very well with someone who took him for Leporello. At first delighted, Leporello suddenly realizes: 'That might have been my wife.' 'All the better', exclaims Giovanni, and laughs immoderately. The voice of the Commendatore rebukes him: 'By dawn you will have laughed for the last time.' His words are declaimed in the tone of an operatic oracle to a wind accompaniment including trombones. After so much dry harpsichord it is deeply disturbing; either in fear or in jest, Leporello observes that it is 'no doubt some voice from the other world'. Giovanni calls out: 'Who's there?' and seeks a living enemy, slashing at the monuments with his sword. The statue speaks again: 'Desist, audacious villain, and leave the dead in peace.' Leporello begins to get nervous, but Giovanni shrugs it off and although he notices the statue, he merely asks Leporello to read the inscription. Feebly protesting that he cannot read by moonlight, Leporello is forced to comply: 'Dell'empio, che mi trasse al passa estremo, qui attendo la vendetta.' 'Here I await vengeance upon the evil man who dragged me to my death.' Now Leporello is really afraid. Giovanni finds it a good joke: 'Vecchio buffonissimo!'. He tells Leporello to invite it to supper, 'or I'll bury you'. **No. 22 DUET** (Leporello: 'O statua gentilissima'). Leporello approaches, recoils, is forced back; Giovanni delights in tormenting him. Finally, emphasizing that it is his master's, not his, invitation, he stammers it out. The statue nods. Leporello recoils, but Giovanni mocks at his terror; only when Leporello demonstrates what he has seen, and Giovanni, looking up, sees the statue nod again, does he cease to be altogether frivolous. In ringing tones he addresses the statue:

'Speak if you can! Shall I see you at supper?' 'Yes.' While Leporello cringes, his master is forced to admit that it is all rather odd ('Bizarra è inver la scena'). But, he cheerfully ends, 'We shall see the good old man at supper. Come, let's go to prepare it.' This movement, one of the gems of the opera, is carried on in the tone of purest *opera buffa*, so that the sudden shudders of supernatural horror, made by changes of harmony and texture without the smallest melodramatic flourish, are all the more effective.

Fourth tableau

[Half stage] A dark room [i.e. dimly lit, in Anna's house].

Scene 12 (Recitative). Having alerted the proper authorities, Ottavio again pleads his cause with Anna. If she seems to spurn him ('O gods! at such a sad moment!') we should recall that it is barely twenty-four hours since her father's death. To his reproach she insists she is not cruel. **No. 23 RECITATIVO OBBLIGATO and ARIA** ('Crudele! ah nò, mio bene'; 'Non mi dir, bell'idol mio'). She desires their union only too much, but the world would look askance. He need say no more; love is his advocate. The tender larghetto of the aria enlarges on this; their roles are reversed, for it is she who asks him to be calm. In the allegretto she looks forward to a happier time ahead. She leaves. (Recitative). Ottavio resolves to help her bear the burden of sorrow.

Fifth tableau

[Full stage] A room in Giovanni's house, with a table set for supper, [The time must be approaching midnight, a good moment for a ghost to walk.]

Scene 13 The rest of the opera is the second **FINALE No. 24. No.24.1** (Allegro vivace. Giovanni: 'Già la mensa è preparata'). He looks forward to a good supper with music; he seems to have forgotten the statue. Servants bring in food; Leporello is starving and, as in Act I, Scene 1, acutely jealous of his master. As he eats Giovanni hears a musical entertainment in three sections. **No. 24.2 TABLE-MUSIC** A small band, of *Harmonie*, of a kind much used for operatic adaptations (oboes, clarinets, horns, bassoons), plays excerpts from recent operatic successes, identified in turn by Leporello. (24.2a) The first extract is from the first finale of *Una cosa rara*, libretto by da Ponte, music by Martin y

Soler. Giovanni seems to be enjoying Leporello's discomfiture. (24.2b) The second extract is a first-act aria from *I due litiganti*, an opera based on Goldoni, music by Giuseppe Sarti. Leporello pours wine, changes the dishes, and snatches a mouthful; Giovanni observes him and decides to catch him out. (24.2c) The third extract is from *Figaro*, inevitably 'Non più andrai'; Leporello remarks that he knows this one just a bit too well.[3] He is caught with his mouth full and is bluffing his way out of trouble when Elvira rushes unceremoniously in. **Scene 14 No. 24.3** (Allegro assai. Elvira: 'L'ultima prova dell'amor mio'). As a last proof of her love she has come to him in pity to bid him repent. She is unable to master her feelings, however, and becomes still less coherent as a result of Giovanni's mock courtesy. She kneels to him; he, having politely risen, kneels too. Leporello murmurs his sympathy for Elvira: 'He has a heart of stone', ready, one may feel, for the man of stone. 'Do not mock me.' 'I, mock you? what do you want, my angel?' 'Change your life!' 'Bravo! Let me eat' (he sits down) 'and you can join me if you like.' Defeated, Elvira resorts to insult, but the trio is dominated at the end by Giovanni's hedonistic exaltation: 'Vivan le femine, viva il buon vino, sostegno e gloria d'umanità!' 'A toast to women, a toast to good wine, support and glory of mankind!' Elvira rushes out in despair. From outside, she screams; then rushes back to escape by another door (there is no change of tempo or orchestration, but a complete change of mood). Leporello is sent to investigate; he too cries out and returns quaking with fear. **No. 24.4** (Molto allegro. Leporello: 'Ah, Signor, per carità'). He gasps out that the stone man is coming with huge strides (which he demonstrates). Giovanni declares that he is mad. Knocking is heard. Leporello refuses to answer it and Giovanni, seeing that his routine threat of violence would be fruitless, picks up a lamp and goes himself. Leporello prudently hides under the table, whence he carries on a frightened commentary on what follows. **Scene 15 No. 24.5** (Andante. Commendatore: 'Don Giovanni, a cenar teco'). The whole orchestra is used for the first time, bringing in this terrible apparition of divine justice with a blast like a hurricane. The statue introduces himself with the opening of the Overture. Giovanni, now forced to believe what is happening, is collected enough to order another meal, but before Leporello has managed to rush off for it the Commendatore speaks again. He cannot now eat mortal food; he has another mission. He speaks with awful slowness; Giovanni urges him to say his piece and Leporello upholds the operatic tradition of analysing the symptoms of his own fear (it is astonishing how, in a sensitive performance, the constant and comical preoccupation of Leporello with himself actually enhances the majesty of the main action). At last the Commendatore continues: 'You invited me to supper. You know your obligation; reply: will you sup with me?' Leporello intervenes to say his master is busy, but Giovanni says he fears nothing, and is resolved to accept. The statue demands his hand as pledge. (*Più stretto*). Its grip freezes Giovanni; he struggles in vain to free himself. The statue's mission is now clear; it is not to avenge, but to warn for the last time:

> Pentiti, cangia vita; è l'ultimo momento.
> Nò, nò, ch'io non mi pento, vanne lontan da me!
> Pentiti, scellerato!
> Nò, vecchio infatuato!

> Repent, change your life; it is your last moment.
> No, no, I'll not repent; get away from me!
> Repent, villain!
> No, old idiot!

One may deplore Giovanni's attitude; but one cannot help but admire his almost superhuman courage. The statue releases him, saying that it is now too late, and leaves. **No. 24.6** (Allegro. Giovanni: 'Da quel tremore insolito'). Only now does he feel fear. Fire starts up all around, and the earth shakes. From beneath, a sombre chorus of demons proclaims that this is but a small punishment for such iniquity. Giovanni cries out; the fire grows and he disappears below. Leporello, seeing and hearing all, echoes his master to the last with a cry of despair. The fire, and the turbulent music with it, subsides. **Scena ultima** [The scene reverts to the room as it was before.] **No. 24.7** (Allegro assai. 'Ah, dov'è il perfido'). The other five characters enter with ministers of justice (mute roles). Anna exclaims that only the sight of Giovanni in chains will satisfy her, but Leporello, crawling out, says his master is far away. With much interruption and coaxing, he gets out enough of the story for the others to understand. 'It is surely the ghost I met', and the others with some awe echo Elvira. **No. 24.8** (Larghetto. Ottavio: 'Or che tutti, o mio tesoro'). Now the threads of ordinary life must be picked up again. Ottavio tries once more to shake Anna's resolve, but she insists on a year's mourning before their marriage; he yields to her wishes and they join in a short, loving duet. Elvira briefly announces that she will retire to a convent; Zerlina and Masetto will go home to celebrate; Leporello is off to the inn to find a better master. The last three join to say:

> Resti dunque quel birbon
> Con Proserpina e Pluton.
> E noi tutti, o buona gente,

Ripetiam allegramente
L'antichissima canzon:

Now let that rotter stay below
With Proserpina and Pluto.
And all of us, good friends, again,
Will join the lively old refrain:

No. 24.9 (Presto. All the characters):

Questo è il fin di chi fà mal,
E de' perfidi la morte alla vita è sempre ugual.

This is the end of the sinner's game;
His life and death are just the same.

The singers are no longer in character, but Mozart allows them to point the moral with the beginning of a double fugue which, if slowed down a little, would reveal its kinship with sacred music. But it develops with electrical brilliance into an *opera buffa* 'chorus' and the opera closes, before the last big chords, with a mocking flicker of fugato from the violins.[4]

3 Don Juan before Da Ponte

EDWARD FORMAN

Da Ponte's account of the speedy composition of the libretto of *Don Giovanni* (see below, p. 122) does little to encourage a pedantic quest for parallels between his libretto and earlier dramatizations of the Don Juan story. He can have had little time for learned research! However, as a serious literary scholar, he was probably already familiar with the major sources, and may have chosen the subject partly because this knowledge enabled him to treat it without time-consuming background reading. Furthermore, he certainly used the libretto by Bertati (see below, p. 35), and internal evidence proves that Bertati referred painstakingly, even slavishly, to literary predecessors, especially Molière. Indirectly, therefore, da Ponte's text reflects material and attitudes from such sources, and thereby falls, almost willy-nilly, into the literary line of descent. But in any case, the Don Juan material was public property: long before da Ponte began to consider the subject, it had achieved independence from purely literary treatment. Modern critics argue that this raises it to the level of 'myth'; in the eighteenth century, it was considered mere fairground entertainment. In Bertati's Prologue, snobbish singers complain indignantly when they are forced, for box-office considerations, to perform such hackneyed stuff. Thus, without reference to any literary texts, da Ponte had adequate access to the outline and main characters of his story. The interaction of the two traditions, literary and popular, enriched the material greatly, and both sides must have influenced da Ponte's instinctive conception of it.[1]

There is little evidence about subliterary presentations which da Ponte may have seen. Performances at fairs or carnivals, by roving actors or puppeteers, were improvised and ephemeral; only rarely did texts or scenarios survive. However, from an overall survey of Don Juan's history before da Ponte, we can piece together a reasonable picture of the popular tradition. Several features of da Ponte's libretto recur frequently within that tradition, but are not found in any of the literary sources. We can only conclude that da Ponte – or at least Bertati – borrowed

27

such features from fairground performances in Italy or Vienna. Neither librettist would have hesitated to incorporate popular material into an *opera buffa*. The most familiar example is the catalogue of Juan's mistresses, a standard feature of popular presentations. Juan's servant would produce a rolled-up list of female names, dangle it amongst the audience, and hint that spectators' wives were mentioned on it. Such an episode occurred in an early Neapolitan Carnival version, in *commedia dell'arte* performances in the 1660s, and in Parisian fairground productions in 1713-14. Bertati, who specialized in catalogue-arias of various kinds, took this obvious opportunity for a set-piece. Da Ponte did no more than improve stylistically on Bertati's version, but it is significant that his aria, one of the most familiar in the opera, derived ultimately from the popular, rather than the literary, tradition.

The 'genealogy' of da Ponte's opening scene can be traced in similar fashion. Again, his direct source was Bertati, but in this case, the sequence did originate in a literary treatment, combining elements from two episodes in Tirso's *El burlador de Sevilla* (see below, 'Literary sources'). In Tirso's opening scene, Isabela, having submitted to a man whom she took to be her fiancé, is horrified when she recognizes Don Juan. Juan's attempt on Ana, and the duel in which her father is killed, take place in Act II. In the libretti of Bertati and da Ponte, these two scenes are fused together, giving the duel its more dramatic position in the opening scene. New features are added – the striking visual effect of the girl struggling to catch a glimpse of Juan's face, and the comic contributions of the terrified servant. These ideas, however, did not originate with the librettists, but were all foreshadowed in one or more of the informal *commedia dell'arte* performances of which records have survived. One of these, the early Neapolitan Carnival version already referred to, begins: 'Isabella enters, clutching Giovanni to find out who he is. He brushes her aside.' Juan's servant contributed little to the episode in this early version, but by the 1660s a troupe of Italian actors based in Paris had given him prominence. The scene was described by the actor who played the part of the servant, Giuseppe Domenico Biancolelli: 'Juan makes his way into the home of the commander Pierre, father of Anna, whom he wished to dishonour. Hearing her cries, the commander arrives, pursuing Juan, who kills him. I improvise some scenes of terror: trying to escape, I fall over the corpse, pick myself up and run off.' This tasteless business was not widely copied, but the servant's part was extended, and a century later we find a closer anticipation of da Ponte in an account published in 1769 by Desboulmiers, on the basis of Italian performances in Paris, which had been frequent since 1743.[2] The Donna Anna material and the death of the commander were moved for the first time into Act I, following a solo scene for the servant. Desboulmiers' description of the sequence could be applied almost as it stands to da Ponte's libretto: 'Juan makes his way into Anna's house, and Arlequin keeps watch at the door. Hearing a noise, he runs off: Anna is calling for help against Juan's attack. . .The fight takes place on stage, the commander is killed and falls after a long struggle against death.'

Such parallels with secondary sources must be placed in an accurate perspective. We cannot suggest that da Ponte or Bertati saw these Parisian performances; but the coincidence of material across a wide range of subliterary versions, over a long period of time, suggests that they may have seen something similar. The fairground performances to which the singers in Bertati's Prologue disparagingly refer may provide a missing link. As Rousset has recently argued, the Don Juan story did depend on such popular forms – even parodies or distortions – for its continuing life and vigour: 'without the masks and tomfoolery of the *commedia dell'arte* performers, Juan's adventures would probably never have reached Molière. . .or Mozart'.[3]

Literary sources

The popular tradition, however much it contributed to the long-term survival of the story, could not have developed without a solid and well-formed foundation. This was provided by a Spanish monk, Gabriel Téllez, under the pseudonym Tirso de Molina. His play, *El burlador de Sevilla y Convidado de piedra (The Trickster of Seville, or The Guest of Stone)*, was first published in 1630, though written some years earlier, perhaps by 1612-16. Tirso may have based his play on some historical or legendary event; he certainly drew on popular ballads, on Jesuit morality plays, and on a handful of dramas from the Spanish Golden Age, featuring animated statues. Out of this material he created a three-act drama, typical of its period in its vigour, complexity, and diversity, although the spectacular 'baroque' elements do not obliterate the sometimes heavy-handed moral message. Tirso's Juan is neither atheist nor voluptuary. He takes more delight in outwitting than in seducing his victims (hence *burlador*, which does not necessarily carry sexual connotations). He claims no immunity from divine justice, but assumes arrogantly that he will eventually obtain divine pardon through the confessional. Some material in Mozart's opera can be traced back to Tirso: the Anna sequence, aspects of Giovanni's relationship with his servant and with the peasants, and elements in the supper scene. These features, however, all passed from *El burlador* into the mainstream of the tradition, and da Ponte could have derived them from intervening sources; there is no clear-cut evidence that he knew Tirso's play. The closest foreshadowing occurs in the final scene, where some of Juan's victims are reunited and paired off, but this is no more than a stereotyped comic ending, and was also used by Goldoni and Bertati.

Tirso's play was soon familiar in Naples, which was still a Spanish territory. Thence it spread to the rest of Italy, and before long Italian adaptations appeared under the title *Il convitato di pietra*. Even the most literary of these reflected the informality and buffoonery associated with *commedia dell'arte*. The earliest extant Italian text is generally, although far from confidently, attributed to Giacinto Andrea Cicognini, and dates from the middle of the seventeenth century. This play is more concise than Tirso's, omitting some minor characters, but incorporating much vulgarity and slapstick. The role of Giovanni's servant has been extended and changed: where Tirso's Catalinón commands a certain degree of admiration for his moral stance, and for his compassion towards his master's victims, Cicognini's Passarino is a gluttonous and treacherous coward, whose principal concern, when Giovanni is struck down, is for his own lost wages. The supernatural element is retained for its spectacular possibilities: Giovanni's torments in Hell are depicted, but the religious implications, which Tirso explored in some depth, are trivialized. There are close textual parallels between the versions of Cicognini and da Ponte. These do not constitute conclusive evidence of direct influence, since they may have been transmitted via the *commedia dell'arte* tradition, but we cannot rule out the possibility that da Ponte knew this play, which even Goldoni acknowledged as the Italian prototype.

The next play of real importance, which overshadows all others of the period, is Molière's *Dom Juan*, produced in Paris in 1665.[4] Although designated *comédie*, it derives some seriousness in moral and social discussion from earlier French tragicomedies, and explores more deeply the emotional reactions of Juan's victims. Molière's Juan amplifies the social *libertinage* displayed by his predecessors: portrayed from the start as 'the would-be spouse of all mankind', he descends, via a declaration of atheism in the central act, to what his servant Sganarelle considers the ultimate depravity, a refined and calculating hypocrisy. The audience's response to him, however, is equivocal: his intellectual superiority, like that of Tirso's Juan, is never in doubt, and often we side with him against his blinkered and gullible victims. The comedy is provided largely by the servant, but also by the peasants, and although it contains an element of slapstick, it is always more refined than in the Italian versions. The play is by far the wittiest and most intellectually stimulating of all da Ponte's possible sources, if not, indeed, of all Don Juan plays. However, these qualities were not universally appreciated, and the play was taken off after a handful of performances. Thereafter, until the 1840s, it was known to the theatre-going public only in a toned-down verse transcription by Thomas Corneille (1677). But Molière's own prose text, less severely expurgated, was published, and both Bertati and da Ponte knew it. Textually, Bertati followed Molière exceptionally closely; and although da Ponte was always freer in his adaptations, he included several verbal echoes not found in Bertati. In each case, the borrowings restore details omitted by Thomas Corneille. Most are connected with the characterization of Elvira, but some features of the peasant sequence and of the supper scene can also be traced to Molière.

The next significant literary treatment was Carlo Goldoni's *Don Giovanni Tenorio, o sia Il dissoluto* (*Don Giovanni Tenorio, or The Debauchee*) (1736). Goldoni was intent upon rescuing the story from the 'unworthy' level of farce to which the popular tradition had consigned it. As a result his play, although not without humour, is almost too cerebral, while his characters, unlike Molière's, have insufficient stature to compensate for the reduction in the spectacular element. It is assumed that da Ponte referred to Goldoni's version, and it would indeed be surprising if he had ignored it. Nevertheless it is easier to pinpoint contrasts than parallels. Goldoni may have influenced the librettist's handling of the Anna–Ottavio–Giovanni relationship, although the betrothed couple, in the play, are positively antagonistic. The 'shepherdess' Elisa, too, responds to Giovanni's advances with more conviction than Zerlina. Moreover, in two major particulars, Goldoni deliberately broke with tradition, omitting Giovanni's servant and altering the dénouement. Da Ponte ignored Goldoni's interesting psychological and dramatic innovations, restoring a standard treatment of these features. Thus whatever influence Goldoni had on details of the libretto, comparison of the texts most strikingly confirms da Ponte's essential desire to follow more familiar presentations.

Subliterary sources

These familiar presentations came from the popular tradition, which had provided a constant counterpoint to literary treatments since the story's first appearance. Amongst the earliest was an interesting Italian scenario, *L'ateista fulminato* (*The Atheist Struck Down*). It is not a Don Juan drama as such; the atheist's name is Aurelio, and although he does ill-treat two ladies, his spiritual sins are given greater emphasis. *L'ateista* is the earliest version in which a Don Juan figure is guilty of religious scepticism and blasphemy, and in this respect, and in the fact that one of Aurelio's victims was abducted from a convent, it fore-shadows Molière.

Other Italian scenarios to have survived from the same period belong to the *commedia dell'arte* tradition. Entitled *Il convitato di pietra*, they resemble Cicognini's play, but go even further in the introduction of clowning and spectacle. Two distinct scenarios have recently been re-printed.[5] Both retain most of Tirso's characters, but combine them with traditional *commedia* figures, including Pollicinella, Zaccagnino and Il Dottore. As in Cicognini, Giovanni's servant plays a prominent part, and a number of other features which are here introduced become ubiquitous within the popular tradition: the opening scene in which Giovanni hides his identity from a distraught victim; the list of his mistresses kept by the servant; and the buffoonery during the supper scene, including a toast by Giovanni 'to the most beautiful woman he had enjoyed in Castille'. All of these features survived to reappear in varying forms in the libretti of Bertati and da Ponte. Italian troupes also performed in Paris during the seventeenth and eighteenth centuries. The best record of their performances is a rough description ('scenario' seems almost too formal a word) by Biancolelli, who played the part of Gio-vanni's servant Arlecchino. The most striking feature of his account is the drastic reduction in size of the cast, which foreshadows eighteenth-century fairground and operatic versions. Tirso and Molière required some twenty named characters, Cicognini sixteen, and Biancolelli only seven, plus unspecified groups of 'villageoises' and 'amoureuses'. As in earlier *commedia* versions, the focus of attention is shifted away from Juan and his victims towards the servant – although here this may mark a bias in the actor's description of his own role. Alongside his cowardice and gluttony, Arlecchino reveals a tendency to moralize. The servant was given this characteristic by Tirso and Molière as well as by Bertati and da Ponte. It is interesting to note this precedent for it in the popular as well as the literary tradition.

Music in association with Don Juan

Music did not play a particularly important role in any of the plays so far considered. Tirso's *El burlador,* in common with many plays of the Spanish Golden Age, was enlivened by a number of songs: villagers frolic to dance-tunes (I.17, II.20); a vocal serenade is performed (II.13); and table-music is heard (III.13, III.20). Most of these *moments musicaux* were retained in the Italian adaptations, but the emphasis on music was greatly reduced in the French versions, and Molière made no specific musical demands. He was deeply interested in stage music and had already collaborated with Lully in a couple of *comédies-ballets,* but may have felt that musical interludes were inappropriate to the relatively serious treatment he had in mind. It is also probable that the shrewd and ambitious Lully would have balked at involvement in such a potentially sensitive production.

The first fully musical treatment of the material, an Italian opera entitled *L'empio punito* (*The Wicked Man Punished*), was performed in spring 1669. The text, by Pippo Acciajoli, was set by Allessandro Melani. Although the protagonist's name is Acrimante, the affinity between the opera and the Don Juan story was soon recognized: while it was in rehearsal, Salvator Rosa looked forward to a new 'opera del Convitato di Pietra'.[6] It is unclear whether later librettists knew this model, but there are some striking textual parallels. Acrimante's servant, Bibi, makes a passing reference to the *'lista'* of his master's conquests (I, 4); and some details of the statue sequences, in the later operatic tradition, may have been influenced by Acciajoli's treatment.

A more interesting musical version of *Le festin de pierre* was performed at the Foire Saint-Germain and other Parisian fairs in 1713-14, and probably on other, less well documented occasions. These *forain* or fairground presentations were in the form known as *comédies en chansons,* popular in France since the previous century, and akin to the contemporary English ballad-opera. Around a simple plot was stitched a patchwork of improvised miming scenes and popular songs. These were incorporated in two ways: a new text appropriate to the play might be performed to a well-known tune, or a catch-phrase or refrain from a familiar song might be fitted into the dialogue. The name le Tellier has been associated with the musical organization of at least one *forain* performance, but nothing more is known of him. The combination of music and spectacle in this lively version was a new element in the Don Juan tradition, and may have provided a crucial transitional link between the seventeenth-century dramatic tradition and subsequent musico-dramatic trends. Apart from the unusual form, the most striking feature of this version is the transfer of attention away from Juan's upper-class victims to the peasants. Like the majority of presentations to date, it portrays two distinct peasant groups, both of whom have long sequences of entertaining frolic before Juan arrives to interrupt their innocent – or not-so-innocent – pleasures. Here, Arlequin produces not only a list of Juan's conquests, but also a large picture depicting some of his exploits. Scenes involving the statue occur in every act, perhaps because the fairground audience's attention could best be retained by constant appeals to sensation. The interest is also kept alive by frequent scene-changes and visual effects, although the balletic element is not as marked as it became in later *forain* theatre.

The following excerpt illustrates the use of music and mime. It is the only scene I have found, before da Ponte, in which Juan's servant deliberately distracts the peasant bridegroom while his master makes advances to the bride. The parallels between this scene and the libretto are by no means close, but the specific idea of using Leporello as a decoy may have come to da Ponte via the popular tradition.

> *Arlequin points out the bride to Juan, who approaches her with extravagant courtesy. Arlequin diverts Pierrot and strikes various attitudes to prevent his seeing his master, who addresses the bride, to the tune* Petite brunette:
> Juan: How this charming creature delights and enchants me! What joy for a lover who can tend the burgeoning shoots of beauty, and water them often!
> *When the song is over, Arlequin leads Pierrot to the side of the stage and tells him to wait, then goes and tells his master, to the tune* Et flon, flon, flon:
> Arlequin: You can help yourself, sir, she's yours.

This presentation may have brought about a change in direction of the Don Juan tradition. Certainly the eighteenth century saw a steady increase in the association of the story with the musical theatre. An anonymous pantomime entitled *Le grand festin de pierre ou L'athée foudroyé* (*The Great Feast of Stone, or The Atheist Struck Down*) appeared in Paris in 1746, but no details have survived – a frustrating loss, since this version must supply a further link in the transition from fairground spectacle to opera proper. The next stage in this transition was ballet: as well as Gluck's score of 1761, there are records of a ballet-interlude performed at the Turin Carnival of 1767, a ballet-pantomime at Kassel in 1770, and two ballets from 1784. An opera on an allied theme, entitled *La pravità castigata* (*Depravity Punished*) (attributed to Angelo Mingotti), was performed in 1734; but the first opera with an established Don Juan title was Callegari's *Il convitato di pietra* (1777). The same year saw performances in Vienna of Righini's three-act tragicomic opera of the same title; it was also performed in Prague, and under Haydn at Esterhàz, and may have been the source of a Polish version set by Albertini in 1783. The *annus mirabilis* for Don Juan operas, however, was 1787, the year not only of Mozart, but of Foppa/ Gardi and Bertati/Gazzaniga as well. Bertati's libretto was certainly the first of these, and provided a direct source for the others. Gardi's opera was produced in deliberate opposition to Gazzaniga's by a rival company in Venice; amongst the features which its librettist borrowed from Bertati are an extended catalogue-aria and a *bouffon* scene in which singers imitate musical instruments. Gardi's Isabella is related to Elvira. His Anna, like Goldoni's, remains infatuated with Giovanni, and delivers ferociously jealous attacks on her rivals.

Bertati and da Ponte

Enough has already been said to indicate the close relationship between the libretti of Bertati and da Ponte. The latter seems never to have acknowledged his debt to a man whom he professed to despise, and no one can deny that he improved the scenes he borrowed beyond recognition. The debt, nevertheless, remains, and in fairness to Bertati we must outline his contribution. From the servant's opening soliloquy until the death of the Commendatore and Giovanni's flight, the two operas follow an identical pattern, but Bertati's Anna describes her adventure to Ottavio at once. Bertati proceeds with an argument between Giovanni and the servant, of a kind common in all the sources: here, as at the beginning of da Ponte's Act II, Giovanni calms the servant down with money. The squabble is interrupted by the arrival of Elvira, whose first scene da Ponte follows closely, although he adds Giovanni's initial failure to recognize Elvira, and deals more neatly with his slipping away, leaving the servant to cope with the troublesome lady. Bertati's next scene involves Ximena, a character whom da Ponte omitted.

A closer relationship returns with the peasant sequence, although Bertati's version is longer. Pasquariello flirts with the bride before the arrival of Giovanni, who deals violently with the bridegroom. Eventually, Giovanni and Maturina are left together, and the seduction follows the traditional pattern. Here, da Ponte parts company from Bertati, who proceeds to a complicated confrontation involving Ximena, Maturina and Elvira, and culminating in a scene of jealous rivalry, with mutual accusations of madness, between Elvira and Maturina. It was based on a hilarious exchange between Molière's two peasant girls, but the active involvement of Elvira is an inconsistency in Bertati's portrayal. Da Ponte retained the madness motif in a modified and reduced form in his first-act quartet.

The rest of Bertati's version is concerned with the statue. Most of the details of the invitation and its acceptance were taken directly from the familiar tradition; but Bertati made one structural change which became the most characteristic feature of both libretti. All the early versions presented a *double* invitation-sequence: the statue visits Juan, but stays only long enough to issue a return invitation, which Juan accepts. In a later scene, he and his servant are regaled by the statue in a ghoulish feast — featuring scorpions, spiders, and vinegar — in a cemetery or tomb. It is on this occasion that he is dragged down to Hell. This pattern, established by Tirso, was followed by all the early Italian versions, including Biancolelli. Molière suppressed the second supper, but still dissociated Juan's final downfall from his entertainment of the statue. Bertati and da Ponte were the only authors to present Giovanni's collapse in his own home. In other respects, too, da Ponte followed Bertati closely, for example in the servant's contribution to the cemetery scene. It was da Ponte's idea to make the statue take the initiative in addressing Giovanni, before the latter had even noticed him. Da Ponte's Act II Scene 12, between Ottavio and Anna, has no counterpart in Bertati, who portrays the supper directly after the invitation. He introduces a second servant for Giovanni, Lanterna, which increases the comic scope. The final visit of Elvira takes place almost at once, and is longer in Bertati than in da Ponte; it is followed by the scene — taken from Molière and retained by da Ponte — in which the servant picks food off his master's plate. Da Ponte's reordering of these events into a continuous finale, so that Elvira's intervention follows this horseplay and leads directly into the statue's arrival, ensures a more dramatic build-up of tension. Finally, the statue arrives, causing much panic among the servants, and deals with the villain swiftly — this section also contains close textual parallels between the two libretti. Bertati follows the Italian and fairground traditions by portraying Giovanni in Hell, before the Epilogue in which, as in da Ponte, everything is explained to the victims, who round things off with a chorus. It should be clear from this summary that da Ponte did take over the outline of most of Bertati's material, although he had to add a lot to it. The quotations in the following pages will demonstrate his stylistic improvements: every scene he adapted shows greater polish, coherence, and wit.

Juan's victims

Having surveyed this long list of da Ponte's sources, we can now investigate more clearly how he used them – both those which he followed directly, and those which indirectly influenced the form in which the material reached him and Mozart. We have already noted the impact of popular traditions on da Ponte's opening sequence, and on the catalogue-aria. We shall now turn to Giovanni's principal female victims, whose 'genealogy' reflects a more complicated mixture of literary and popular sources.

Although Anna's adventure draws on two episodes in Tirso, she herself is quite unlike Tirso's ladies, Isabela and Ana. Both these are indeed tricked by the *burlador*, but neither escapes severe moral censure. Both are only too ready to receive male visitors: their horror springs not from Juan's actions, but from his identity. There has been controversy amongst Tirso scholars, as amongst some students of the opera, about the success or failure of Juan's attempt on Ana. There are arguments which apply to both works, notably the suggestion that her reaction is so ferocious because Juan succeeded in seducing her. In the case of *El burlador,* defenders of her chastity currently hold the fort, but their main arguments cannot be transferred directly to the opera. Tirso's Juan actually admits his failure, and the playwright makes this admission the basis of a reconciliation between Ana and her lover; and while Juan's claim may be suspect, Tirso would scarcely have allowed his happy ending to depend on a misunderstanding or deception. There may be some significance in da Ponte's refusal to tie everything up so neatly, but the differences in his presentation are so fundamental that no detailed cross-application of arguments is really feasible.

Ana does not appear on stage in Tirso's version, although her off-stage shrieks are heard. In the early Italian scenarios, she contributes slightly more, delivering a lament over her father's corpse, and asking the King to help in her quest for vengeance. Biancolelli followed Tirso in allowing Anna to be heard but not seen; Molière and the *forain* writers ignored her altogether. Goldoni's Anna is a complex character, who continues to respond to the fascination of Giovanni even after his murder of her father; a similar complexity emerges from the Romantic interpretation of Mozart's opera, although this can scarcely be justified with reference to the libretto (see below, pp. 59 and 83). Bertati gave Anna prominence in his opening sequence, but thereafter she retires to a convent, leaving Ottavio to pursue the still unidentified assailant. Anna herself does not appear again. Her role is more extended in Righini's opera, where, however, she seeks vengeance from Don Alfonso, a figure derived from Goldoni's King, rather than Ottavio. Da Ponte neglected this example and instead, after using Bertati's opening sequence, developed the psychological and dramatic impact of Anna's character with some originality, and allowed her to join Giovanni's other victims in active pursuit of him.

Elvira's origins are even mistier than Anna's. She bears a superficial similarity to Tirso's Isabela, who follows Juan from Naples to Seville, intending to force herself upon him in marriage. This Isabella reappears in Goldoni, and in Righini's opera, but there is no indication that she feels the deep passion for Giovanni which, in Molière's Elvire, becomes a disinterested, religious emotion. Molière's presentation may also owe something to *L'ateista fulminato*, in which Leonora is abducted from a convent and later abandoned. Molière gave her a new name, and enriched her character greatly. She has only two scenes, but both are crucial, and both recur in modified forms in Bertati and da Ponte. Her initial vigorous indignation over Juan's treatment of her (Molière I.3, Bertati scs. 6-8, da Ponte I.5) gives way to a moving appeal to him to alter his impious life-style before it is too late (Molière IV.6, Bertati sc. 22, da Ponte II.14). Her role, like Anna's, was extended by da Ponte, and more fully integrated as a result of her association with Giovanni's other victims.

In his adaptation of Molière's text, Bertati gave a very close, often literal, translation; da Ponte, on the other hand, showed originality and independence. One example of this is provided by the servant's attempt to defend Giovanni's conduct. Bertati's Pasquariello produces an uncharacteristic learned reference:

Alessandro il Grande non era giammai sazio di far nuove conquiste; il mio padrone, se avesse ancora cento spose, e cento, sazio non ne saria, nè mai contento; egli è il grande Alessandro delle femmine.

Alexander the Great never tired of making fresh conquests; if my master had another hundred wives, and a hundred more, he would not be tired, nor ever satisfied; he is the Great Alexander of women.

This introduces the catalogue-aria neatly, but dramatically it is tame, and the text is too laboured to be witty. Bertati is trying to retain a joke which worked well for Molière, but which cannot readily be transferred to the context of opera. In Molière's play, the parallel with Alexander was eloquently drawn by Juan himself before Elvire arrived (I.2); and when Sganarelle is put on the spot by Elvire, all he can manage to stammer out is 'Madame, les conquérants, Alexandre et les autres mondes sont causes de notre départ.' ('Madam, conquering heroes, Alexander and the other worlds brought about our departure.') Molière here combines two comic effects: the contrast between Juan's eloquence and his servant's incoherence, and Elvire's frustration at receiving a nonsensical explanation. Bertati sticks closely to his source, but destroys both these effects. Da Ponte ignores the details of Molière's exchange, but restores its spirit, giving the tongue-tied Leporello an ideal formula for musical setting: 'Madama, veramente, in questo mondo con-cios-sia-cosa-quando-fosse-che il quadro non è tondo!' ('Madam, truly, in this world, inasmuchas-this-or-that-however-it-might-be, a square is not round!')

When Elvira interrupts Giovanni's supper, shortly before the statue arrives, Bertati copied Molière even more closely. Her moving moral appeal was an integral part of Molière's presentation of Juan's gradual descent into hypocrisy and blasphemy; but it is hard to justify Bertati's retention of this long digression within the farcical spectacle which ends his *opera buffa*. A few lines from the climax of Elvire's speech will confirm how faithfully Bertati translated the French text:

Je vous ai aimé avec une tendresse extrême . . . et toute la récompense que je vous demande, c'est de corriger votre vie . . . je vous le demande avec larmes; et si ce n'est assez des larmes d'une personne que vous avez aimée, je vous en conjure par tout ce qu'il y a de plus capable pour vous toucher.

Ah, in ricompensa di tanto amor ch'ebbi per voi, non chiedo che il vostro pentimento . . . sì vi scongiuro colle lagrime agli occhi, per quell'amor, che per me aveste un giorno, per quel ch'è più capace di toccar il cor vostro.

I have loved you so tenderly/much, and all I ask in return is that you amend your life/repent. With tears in my eyes I beg, by the love you once felt for me, (or) by whatever is better able to move you/your heart.

All this – and a good deal more along similar lines – is reduced by da Ponte to a few preliminaries, and a single line of substance: 'Che vita cangi!' ('Change your life!') Da Ponte's (or Mozart's) overall presentation of Elvira may gain resonance and pathos from its association with Molière's portrayal, but here the reduction of an eloquent appeal to a single rather hysterical command seems dismissive, if not comic. This reaction is confirmed a moment later, when Elvira rushes across the stage in terror after her confrontation with the statue – an indignity which neither Molière nor Bertati made her undergo.

One other detail in da Ponte's treatment of Elvira is of interest. When she first recognizes Giovanni, she delivers a long recitative account of her adventures and grudges, to which Leporello responds with the aside 'Pare un libro stampato' ('Like a printed book'). This unusual simile is a direct reminiscence of Molière – it was not retained by Thomas Corneille, nor copied by Bertati – but da Ponte has altered its context. In

Molière's play, it was applied by Sganarelle to Juan himself, after the latter's eloquent defence of sexual infidelity. Molière stressed the intellectual gulf between Giovanni and his servant more than any other interpreter of the story, and Sganarelle is moved to admiration by his master's powers of expression: 'Good heavens, how you churn it out! You seem to have learned all that by heart, and you talk just like a book!'

The portrayal of Juan's peasant victims shows greater continuity. Tirso presented two, a fisher-girl who helps Juan after his shipwreck, and a peasant bride. Both girls are given a promise of marriage by Juan, and on that basis are very happy to succumb to his advances. The Italian versions retained both these sequences, incorporating the list episode into the former. The French classical plays retained two peasant girls, but combined them in a single sequence. The *forain* versions of 1713-14 restored the fisher-girl to her independent position, and gave all the rustics greater prominence. Bertati was the first to omit the shipwreck (and with it the fisher-girl) altogether. The event had not been without significance, being presented as preliminary divine warning that Juan could not continue his life-style with impunity, but Bertati could not find space for it in a one-act opera. Within this shifting framework, a surprising number of details survived, almost unchanged, in many versions, including da Ponte's. In most, for example, a gibe is made about the proverbial inconstancy of noble gentlemen, although da Ponte was the first to give Giovanni the witty rejoinder 'Eh, un impostura della gente plebea.' ('That's a slander by the lower classes.') In most versions, too, Juan flatters his victim, suggesting that she is too beautiful to be 'wasted' on her bridegroom. Tirso's Juan praises Aminta, saying 'You have hands too beautiful for the wife of a peasant.' The emphasis on her hands may have a special significance, to which we shall return, but the general form of this compliment seems to have become almost traditional. Molière included a more elaborate version (II.2) which Bertati all but translated:

E voi con quegli occhietti così belli, con quel bocchin di rose, quella sì cara mano, darete ad un villano? No, mia dolcezza, no. Voi meritate un assai miglior stato.

And you, with such beautiful little eyes, such rosy lips, such a dear hand, will you give yourself to a villager? No, my sweet, no. You deserve a much better position.

Da Ponte's version combines ideas from several of these sources:

Vi par che un onest'uomo. . .possa soffrir, che quel visetto d'oro, quel viso inzuccherato, da un bifolcaccio vil sia strappazzato?. . .Voi non siete fatta per esser paesana, un'altra sorte vi procuran quegli occhi bricconcelli. . .

Do you think a gentleman can allow this precious, honeyed, little face to be insulted by a servile boor?. . .You weren't made to be a peasant, these roguish eyes will win you a different lot.

I have already quoted Juan's compliment, in Tirso, to the girl's hands. In the same scene, he tries to hold her hand, but she refuses. However, in the following act, when he is on the point of seducing her, he asks a second time for her hand, saying 'give me this hand, and let our vows be confirmed by it'. This moment, directly or indirectly, surely provided the ultimate source for 'Là ci darem la mano'. The handclasp itself was of crucial significance for Tirso, who made it a *Leitmotiv* of his play. Handclasping is associated with critical moments of Juan's crimes and punishment. He holds hands with Isabela (I.1), Tisbea (I.16), and Aminta (II.22, III.8) – in each case drawing attention to the action in his words. When, therefore, the statue asks for *Juan's* hand on two separate occasions (III.14, III.20), a clear visual parallel is provided which firmly establishes the connection between Juan's misdemeanours and his final doom.

Tirso, indeed, went one stage further in establishing this connection. In the most elaborate of his handclasping scenes, that with Aminta (III.8), Juan's promise of fidelity culminates with the words: 'If perchance my word or my faith fail you, I pray to God that by treachery or perfidy I may be murdered by a man – but a dead one – God forbid he should be alive!' This final aside is no more than a clumsy, childish attempt by Juan to annul the effect of his oath by means of a mental reservation. From Tirso's point of view, however, such a speech not only gave him an 'excuse' for the spectacular intervention of the statue, but also placed greater emphasis on the moral fitness of the conclusion: not only does God dispense justice, however tardily, He also 'plays the game' by complying with terms laid down by the culprit. The early Italian versions make this point even more clearly by substituting 'a stone man' for 'a dead man' in the fraudulent oath. Even Goldoni, although he eliminated the active intervention of the statue, retained a similar exchange:

Giovanni: I swear by the divinity which rules heaven and earth: you shall be my wife.
Elisa: And if you fail?
Giovanni: Then let a thunderbolt fall from heaven, and my treacherous soul fall into the abyss.

(Dent quotes this scene more fully as a 'distinct anticipation' of 'Là ci darem',[7] but it is no closer to da Ponte's text than many other potential sources.) In every case, as Giovanni seduces the peasant girl, he invites, in the context of a solemn oath, the precise fate which will eventually overtake him. The librettists must have known about this element in the tradition, although Bertati omitted even the handclasp. Perhaps da Ponte wished on principle to reduce the level of moral (or pseudo-moral) discussion; perhaps he felt that such a specific ironic detail could not easily be transferred to opera. It is at any rate interesting that the one feature which he did retain was the striking visual one of the handclasp, providing the obvious parallel with the play's dénouement.

Juan's downfall

Juan's downfall and death, whether they take place at the commander's tomb, in Juan's house, or in the open, were dealt with in a standard manner by virtually every author. The statue confirms his reciprocal invitation to Juan, asks for his hand as a pledge of good faith, then drags him off in a firm, icy grasp. There are strong textual parallels between da Ponte's libretto and the early Italian play by Cicognini. This version is seldom suggested as a direct source for da Ponte, but it stands at the head of the popular tradition which influenced him greatly. Cicognini's treatment of Giovanni's final moments runs:

Statua: Don Giovanni, dammi la mano.
Giovanni: Eccola; ma, oh Dio, che stringo un ghiaccio, un freddo marmo? Lasciami, traditore!
  Don Giovanni pone mano a uno stile, e gli tira nel petto.
Statua: Pentiti, Don Giovanni.
Giovanni: Lasciami dico, ohimè.
Statua: Pentiti, Don Giovanni.
Giovanni: Ohimè io moro, aiuto!
Statua: Pentiti, Don Giovanni.
  Qui precipita Don Giovanni.

Statue: Don Giovanni, give me your hand.
Giovanni: Here it is; but, oh God! what an icy, stony grip! Let me go, traitor!
  Giovanni seizes a dagger and strikes him in the chest.
Statue: Repent, Don Giovanni.
Giovanni: Leave me, I say, ah!
Statue: Repent, Don Giovanni.
Giovanni: Alas, I'm dying, help!
Statue: Repent, Don Giovanni.
  Here Don Giovanni collapses.

Some of Giovanni's exclamations and the triple call to repentance by the statue were paralleled exactly by da Ponte. The latter detail, so memorable in Mozart's setting, is not found in Tirso, and deserves further comment.

Part of Tirso's moral point was that such last-minute repentance could *not* be offered by the statue. His Juan never doubts that he will one day be called to account for his misdeeds: his defiance of moral standards is based not on a sense of immunity, still less on religious scepticism, but on the notion that there is plenty of time for repentance, confession, and absolution. Whenever he is warned that his sins will eventually catch up with him, he simply retorts 'Tan largo me lo fiáis!' ('You give me such long credit!') This remark is so frequently repeated as to become a catch-phrase, and was even used as the title of one edition of Tirso's play. Juan's attitude, however, is specifically rejected by the statue, whose moral message is that last-minute repentance, or conversion 'under duress', cannot atone for a life of hardened sin, particularly if confession is postponed through deliberate calculation. Interestingly enough, this moral is presented in a musical setting, as the background to the macabre supper scene in the temple. The statue's provision of music balances Juan's own table-music at the earlier meal, but his text is a pointed criticism of Juan's oft-repeated opinion: 'While in the world of the living, it is not right that anyone should say, "What long credit you give me! ", for the time for encashment comes so quickly.' A few moments later, Juan, realizing he has no hope of escape, actually asks for a chance to confess, but the statue refuses unequivocally, and adds sternly, 'This is God's justice: as you behave, so you must pay.'

This uncompromising message has been quoted fully in order to emphasize the degree to which it was watered down in subsequent versions. Juan never avoids punishment, but in the Italian and French plays, and in the operas, the chance of escape is held out to him again and again, by Elvira as well as by the statue. Molière retained the idea of postponed repentance, but turned it into a whimsical joke. After Elvire's impassioned plea, Juan astounds Sganarelle by pretending to take matters seriously:

Juan: Sganarelle, we ought to be thinking of reform, all the same.
Sganarelle: You don't say!
Juan: Yes, indeed we must reform. Another twenty or thirty years of this life, then we'll take thought for ourselves.

This was translated word for word by Bertati, so da Ponte must have made a conscious decision to omit even this trite reference to Tirso's weighty message. It would be rash to deduce from this that the licentious abbé wished to convince himself or anyone else that it was never too late to obtain absolution; but it does indicate his desire – shared with earlier Italian dramatists of the story (including Bertati) – to concentrate on the spectacular side of Giovanni's punishment, rather than on its implications for his own life, or his spectators'. As Mandel put it, 'on the philosophical or moral side, da Ponte is not likely to give anyone a headache'; and I have analysed the moral precepts of his predecessors not in order to show that his message is different, but rather to suggest that, compared to some of them, he scarcely has a clear-cut message at all (see also below, p. 88).

I have concentrated in this chapter almost entirely on what da Ponte borrowed from earlier dramatists. This should not be taken as implying criticism: the true test of originality, as Auden pointed out, is not how little an author borrows, but how inimitable he himself is; and the fact that almost every historian of the Don Juan story has considered the opera to be a major turning-point must owe something to the shifts in emphasis, characterization, and moral brought about by the librettist. The quotations used above illustrate, at least in part, da Ponte's skill in versification and in the composition of witty and lively dialogue. Large portions of the opera, of course, owe nothing to the sources, but were original contributions. Some of these, particularly in Act II, have come in for criticism. It may be fairer, however, to end this chapter by singling out the Act I finale as da Ponte's most successful invention. It is quite unlike anything in the sources; its suitability for the operatic context is at once apparent; and it contributes to his main structural innovation, the unification of the plot, achieved by allowing all Giovanni's enemies to join forces against him. This simple, apparently obvious, device would not have appealed to the baroque originators of the story, but was essential if their episodic treatment was to be converted into a classical structure, and it says much for da Ponte's formal control that he was able to achieve this while working from such a disparate set of sources.

4 The libretto

Structure

The principal problem of da Ponte's libretto may be expressed in the common opinion that it is a loose string of episodes without organic development. This opinion was held by Dent (in *Mozart's Operas*) and Newman, whose chapter on *Don Giovanni* (*More Opera Nights*) is a sustained attack on da Ponte, informed by great critical intelligence, but overstated and sometimes based on false premises. Newman and Abert (*Mozart's Don Giovanni*) shared a surprisingly high opinion of Bertati, and attribute da Ponte's failures to the need to pad out a plot too short for his purposes. But Bertati's *Don Giovanni* is just a shorter string of loosely connected episodes; and that this is the proper, as well as the normal, mode of handling this subject is underlined by the failure of Goldoni to turn it into a well-made play. One might argue that the succinct one-act form, occasioned by his *Don Giovanni*'s being the second part of a *capriccio drammatico*, should have assisted Bertati in producing something more closely knit. But he has too many women; his Anna does nothing, his Ximena hardly more, his Maturina (Zerlina) is a trivial figure, and her Biagio a nonentity (as Masetto is not). Ximena and Maturina yield to Giovanni without much doubt or interruption. Elvira, who is largely Molière's creation, is treated foolishly by Bertati; far from being humiliated by a slanging-match with Maturina (as Abert suggests), she returns insult for insult as if she were of peasant stock herself, and Gazzaniga's music underscores this inappropriate equality. Even Ottavio is much more fully developed by da Ponte, and if Giovanni and Pasquariello/Leporello are essentially the same figures, they benefit from da Ponte's far livelier wit. As for the peasant couple, Abert noted da Ponte's achievement:

Da Ponte endowed [Zerlina] with innocent grace and with the natural impulsiveness of a simple country girl. One happy inspiration of da Ponte's was her reconciliation with Masetto . . . Bertati's Biagio appears only once, just to witness Maturina's unfaithfulness and then to be thrashed off the stage by Don Giovanni. Masetto's martyrdom is longer

45

and more painful, but for this reason Zerlina's return to him seems more convincing.[1]

Abert exaggerates when he concludes that the peasants are not really comical, and that Leporello alone is a *buffo* character; we may laugh even at Elvira without impropriety, and Giovanni himself is a comic character – much of the time. Nevertheless he admirably expresses da Ponte's main achievement, which is the inter-connection of the characters. Bertati's libretto is a sketchy affair; da Ponte's, for all its problems of timing and movement, contains in embryo the living creatures who are born of Mozart's music. Da Ponte's intrigue, considering the nature of his sources, is remarkably tight; it is found wanting only by comparison with *Figaro*, whose origins are a single and brilliant theatrical work.

Even the admittedly loose elements in da Ponte's structure are susceptible of a certain amount of rationalization, which may take the form of a structural analysis of the libretto, or of explanation of points left unclear during the rapid, laconic action by means of reference to the sources such as Tirso, Molière, or Bertati.

Christof Bitter has pointed to a clarity and symmetry in da Ponte's structure, in which both acts bring Giovanni's antagonists together from a position of separation.[2] In Act II this separation is partly the result of Giovanni's machinations, since the exchange of clothes with Leporello leads to the deceit of Elvira and the beating of Masetto. It is this section which is often held to demonstrate da Ponte's helplessness when he was forced to fall back on his own invention. Jahn detected 'coarseness' here, and Abert complained that 'the second act could certainly have done with some new dramatic motive, for the continued pursuit of Don Giovanni hardly appears enough to maintain the tension . . . To put together his second act [da Ponte] had recourse to such hackneyed expedients of opera buffa as exchanging clothes and engineering scuffles. . .' Dent even refers to 'confusion of plot, redeemed only by the beauty of Mozart's music'.[3] It is of course no defence to ask what else da Ponte might have done. In fact, he ingeniously mingles comedy with seriousness. The beating of Masetto gives rise to the reconciliation which Abert rightly praised; the scene with the sextet is a marvellous intermingling of *parti serie, buffe,* and *di mezzo carattere*; the trio acquires an unearthly beauty from the blend of Elvira's pathetic retreat, Giovanni's impassioned hypocrisy, and Leporello's stifled laughter. Of course these things exist fully only in the music, but their seeds are in the text. The first half of Act II shows the futility of merely human endeavour against Giovanni, and thus leads naturally to the graveyard scene. Da Ponte then cut Bertati's supper scene to essentials, reordered its events so that Elvira's entry immediately precedes that of the statue, and formed it, to its inestimable advantage, as a continuous finale.

The parallel structure of the acts includes their starting with exterior sets, with interiors at the end (within the first finale, and before No. 23). The parallelism is most easily presented in tabular form; Table 1, partly based on Bitter, can of course only apply to the original version (Prague, 1787).

Table 1. *Parallel structure of the acts*

ACT I		ACT II	
Nos. 1-7		Nos. 14-18	
SEPARATE EXPOSITION		SEPARATION OF ANTAGONISTS	
[Giovanni and three women]		[Giovanni disguised or absent]	
ANNA	Giovanni–Anna		Giovanni–Leporello
	DEATH of Commendatore		DECEIT of Elvira
	(Trio)		(Trio)
	Anna–Ottavio (Duet)		
ELVIRA	Misdirected towards	Elvira misdirected towards Leporello	
	Leporello (No. 4)		
ZERLINA	Giovanni–Masetto		Giovanni–Masetto
	Giovanni–Zerlina		Zerlina–Masetto
Nos. 8-10		Nos. 19-21	
MIXTURE OF PERSONS AND		MIXTURE OF PERSONS AND	
PASSIONS; beginning of collective		PASSIONS; collective antagonism	
antagonism		misdirected to Leporello	
QUARTET		SEXTET	
[Giovanni retires to background]		[Leporello escapes]	
ANNA convinced of Giovanni's guilt		OTTAVIO convinced of Giovanni's guilt	
Aria (No. 10)		Aria (No. 21)	
		[Graveyard scene]	
Leporello's narrative		Giovanni's narrative	
Aria (No. 11)		Duet (No. 22)	
[Giovanni's garden]		[Anna's house]	
Aria (No. 12)		Aria (No. 23)	
FINALE	Entry of maskers	FINALE	Entry of Elvira
	Attempt on Zerlina		Retribution: the statue
	Collective antagonism		Collective conclusion

To accept the parallel is not altogether to deny the episodic nature of the result in performance. Act I has thirteen numbers of the twenty-four, but only four tableaux of the nine. Elements which correspond in position do not necessarily correspond in importance. Giovanni's outrages at the opening of Act II are trivial indeed compared to those which open Act I, and his rather subdued blasphemy (graveyard scene) has no direct parallel. Nor does Ottavio's belated conviction of Giovanni's guilt match Anna's in importance. These facts, however, must be considered against another pattern: the move from night, through dawn (second tableau), the middle of the day (the rest of Act I) and twilight (Act II, No. 15) to night again (by No. 19). Giovanni's most heinous crimes are done in the night; he makes a brutal attempt on Anna and kills her father instead of escaping. His midday offences are comparatively light; he tricks Elvira at dawn and twilight, and he makes his attempt on Zerlina's virtue in the first finale, doubtless believing her, after 'Là ci darem', to be willing. With night comes his irreligious frivolity in the graveyard, and his death. Thus counterpointed by a ternary or arch form, the binary parallel is not exact; but it is not unimpressive for an apparently hasty improvisation on a hoary old theme.

Of course, such structural rationalization is not itself an adequate rebuttal of the accusation of a falling-off in the second act from the high comedy with tragic elements of the first. One might suggest that it should simply be enjoyed as a display of virtuosity: da Ponte's, Mozart's, or Giovanni's. Nevertheless there is a structural flaw in Act II which it is useless to deny. In the nineteenth century *Don Giovanni* was sometimes played in more than two acts. The justifications for thus flouting the clear intention of the authors are the great length of *Don Giovanni*, the four-act structure of *Figaro*, and the sextet No. 19. The latter is unmistakably in the form of a miniature finale with all the main elements of a longer one: the growth in number of characters from two (singing separately) to two pairs, ignorant of each other's presence, to five singers (Leporello silent, Elvira pleading with four others), to six, but with Leporello against the five. This last phase is in a faster tempo and is dramatically static, like the end of nearly every multi-movement finale; despite its surface speed it has little musical action, being, as Charles Rosen says in his admirable analysis, 'nothing more than a series of tonic (V–I) cadences in E flat, dramatized, decorated, expanded, and fantastically enlivened'; it has, in fact, a musical function to fulfil 'almost in spite of the words, for "Mille torbidi pensieri" hardly implies so rigid an attachment to the tonic'.[4] But despite this pronounced and unmistakable finale-character, the sextet is not even the end of a scene or tableau. An original plan may well have been to have Leporello escape in the coda; the final act might then begin in the graveyard, followed by the Anna–Ottavio scene and the finale. But this is speculation. What is certain is that the scenes following the sextet gave considerable trouble, and it was there that the major alterations were made for Vienna.[5] Funny as it is, the escape of Leporello occupies more than enough time even in the Prague version for so negative an episode, and in the Vienna version he has to escape twice, which is not an improvement.

The problem does not end there, for a first finale is not so easily found as a third. Dent believed that Act I would have ended, like that of *Figaro*, with an aria, 'Or sai chi l'onore'. Another end might have been the preceding quartet; but Mozart did not compose it in a finale-like structure, and its action arouses the intense suspicion of Anna and leads directly to her 'Don Ottavio, son morta' (No. 10). No. 11, 'Fin ch'an dal vino', would be too short and leave the second act nothing but finale. If No. 10 ended the act the next scene (Ottavio's recitative, I.14) could be omitted, and the second act begin like the third with a master–servant dialogue (I.15). But, as Dent realized, a major question is raised by any of these solutions: where, in a four-act plan, would the tenor have an aria? The question is less trivial than it seems, and may have led to a change in the whole design. Ottavio is not a *buffo* like the tenor in *Figaro* who doubles Basilio and Curzio and who hardly needs an aria; he is an *opera seria* figure to whom Bertati had given a long aria to end the first tableau. Da Ponte and Mozart ended that scene much more effectively with a duet, and when Anna has told her story (I.15) it is, rightly, she who has the aria. In the Vienna version 'Dalla sua pace' was inserted here, an anti-climax after Anna's great cry for vengeance that has often worried critics. At Prague the aria was 'Il mio tesoro' and was placed after the sextet; the only other time Ottavio is alone on stage is between 'Non mi dir' and the second finale, where an aria would be disastrously out of place. On the whole the balance of probability favours Dent's theory, but the difficulty of dividing Act I is a tribute to da Ponte, for it is remarkably well sewn together. Act II may perhaps abide our question.[6]

Time and place in *Don Giovanni*

The time-scale of the action, and the places at which it unrolls, have often been misunderstood. The facts are simple: the action of *Don Giovanni* covers approximately twenty-four hours, and there are nine tableaux, alternately requiring full and half stage to facilitate scene-changing. Da Ponte demanded much intense activity from his characters and packed it into the traditional dramatic time-span so that *Don Gio-*

vanni is, like *Figaro, une folle journée* – the true title of Beaumarchais' *Le mariage de Figaro* and the name by which, as Mozart remarked in his letter to Jacquin of 15 October 1787, his own *Figaro* was known in Prague. As the characters put it in the sextet: 'Che giornata o stelle, è questa! Che impensata novità!' 'Heavens, what a day this is! what an unforeseen event!') Yet Benn, in *Mozart on the Stage*, lays out the action over four or five days, which would certainly encourage the view that Ottavio is unduly leisurely in the pursuit of justice.[7] He gives no evidence for thus crediting da Ponte with a worthless innovation in dramatic structure, and like other misinterpretations his partly depends on the unfounded idea that there is a scene-change, from street to countryside, before No. 5. Da Ponte places the second tableau in the street, and extends it from before No. 3 to after No. 11. It begins in darkness and ends in full daylight; there is plenty of action and no danger of monotony. The mere presence of peasants seems to have led to the notion that half the scene is in the country, and Newman takes unfair advantage of this error in his critique of da Ponte's craftsmanship.[8] Bertati has his central sequence in the country without the city walls; but that is no excuse for appearing to believe that da Ponte brings Anna and Ottavio out on a country stroll in search of a murderer. It follows that Giovanni does not have a country house, as is often stated, but a town house. In Bertati's country scene there are cottages (*case rustiche*), one of which belongs to Maturina, and a handsome villa (*nobile casino*) belonging to Ximena. In da Ponte, Giovanni's house is often absurdly translated 'palace' or even 'castle'. He himself once calls it *palazzo*, but only to impress the peasants (I.8). When addressing his social equal, Anna (I.12), he uses an exact word: *casa*, house. To Leporello he uses the diminutive *casino*, perhaps jokingly as it has the double meaning of 'villa' and 'brothel'; but that brothel is not the only meaning, as Moberly assumes, is shown by Bertati's use of it for Ximena's house.[9] *Casino* also appears in da Ponte's stage-directions after 'Là ci darem'. To Zerlina, Giovanni uses *casinetto*, a mock-diminutive (of 'villa', surely, not 'brothel'), to reassure her. The peasants, therefore, have come to town on a spree. Masetto sings in No. 5: 'poco dura de'matti la festa' – the holiday is short, enjoy it to the full. The town, incidentally, is never named, but is probably not meant to be Seville. Tirso's settings include Naples, Seville and the country; Molière's is Sicily; Bertati's is Villena in Aragon, which is still a good distance from Elvira's town of Burgos.

Another common and equally gratuitous scene-change is introduced into Act I in order to convert 'Fin ch'an dal vino' into a sort of set-piece, a credo. Thus Act I Scene 15 has been staged in the ballroom (so that a change is needed to the garden for the next scene and back again during the finale); in a private room (a new set), with Giovanni being dressed for the feast, drinking champagne and prodigally throwing away the glass (the name 'champagne-aria' derives from this superfluous stage-business and from early German translations which dragged in this un-Spanish wine); or even in the garden, surrounded by picnicking peasants. None of this makes any sense if da Ponte's words are used, since the preceding recitative is obviously a street meeting, in which Giovanni is told by Leporello what has been going on in his own home – hardly necessary if he were already there. Preferable to this multiplication of scenes would be a simple economy whereby the second tableau of Act I (which might legitimately be a square rather than a narrow street) would serve for the first of Act II; both are full-stage scenes near Elvira's lodging. The first scene of Act I and the second of Act II could also be the same, since both are half-stage, confined spaces pertaining to Anna's house.

The twenty-four-hour cycle may require some explanation. Anna, in her narrative (I.13), says that the night was by no means young when the intruder entered her room ('Era già alquanto avanzata la notte'), and Leporello ('Notte e giorno faticar') gives us the impression that he would rather be in bed. Still, for a young girl and a tired servant midnight is late, and the action may plausibly be considered to begin about then, with the servants and Commendatore in bed and unconscious of Anna's first cries for help. A good and positive improvement upon Bertati is that Anna only tells Ottavio what happened the next morning, when she is collected enough, and when it has become useful to do so; but she does not, as Benn would have it, wait as long as thirty-six hours. The next events take place at dawn; it should probably be dark enough for Elvira, when she enters, not to be too obviously recognizable.[10] Either Giovanni and Leporello have not gone to bed, or they are up early because, as Leporello deduces, an amorous adventure is afoot, of which, however, we hear nothing more; it is perhaps a residue of Bertati's Ximena, whom da Ponte wisely omitted, and thus an oversight of the librettist's, although it shows how unceasingly Giovanni plays the game. The peasants arrive later in the morning (time may well seem to elapse at this point), and Giovanni invites them to make merry at his house and garden. The third tableau is indeed a *déjeuner sur l'herbe* and the hiding in niches, and masking, are daylight activities. The first act ends in early afternoon.

Act II begins a few hours later; as Elvira comes out onto the balcony

the twilight beauty matches the softening of her mood. Night falls —
the trio is headed 'Si fà notte a poco a poco' — and it is soon dark
enough for Giovanni and Leporello to be mistaken for each other.
When Anna and Ottavio reach home (presumably after a visit to the
grave) it is quite dark, at least in the courtyard overshadowed by the
house (II.7); the moon may have risen, making the 'bujo loco' still more
frighteningly dark by contrast. The moon shines in full splendour on
the graveyard, for Leporello manages to read by it.

The existence of a statue of the Commendatore (not necessarily
equestrian; the stage-direction is ambiguous on this point), complete
with menacing inscription, may seem to try the twenty-four-hour time-
scale severely. Da Ponte does not trouble to explain; the statue was a
sine qua non of the subject. The literary sources suggest that Anna's
father was a man of great distinction, to whom a statue has been erected
in his lifetime, so that the first oddity is that it should be in this 'Loco
chiuso, in forma di sepolcreto' rather than in a public square.[11] As for
the inscription, Bertati actually shows Ottavio instructing a sculptor,
who apparently engraves something different in detail from what he is
told, or at least from what Giovanni shortly afterwards reads out. Da
Ponte rightly omitted this scene as otiose. It has been suggested that
Anna and Ottavio are returning from inspecting the inscription when
they enter in Act II Scene 7. But rationalization of the inscription
seems out of place. If a statue can speak and nod, then an inscription
can appear supernaturally to warn the miscreant; it may not 'really'
have been there at all.

The major problem here is Giovanni's remark earlier in the scene:
'È tardi? [guarda sul orologio] Oh, ancor non sono due della notte.'
This could obviously mean 'not yet 2 a.m.', but in that case it is odd
even for Giovanni to say 'Is it late?. . . No, not yet 2 o'clock'. It is
usually suggested that he means 'Two hours into the night' or two after
sunset. Gresser, in an article on the 'due della notte' question, points to
a libretto translated into English by da Ponte's son and published in
New York in the librettist's lifetime (1826), which has Giovanni say 'Oh
no! not two o'clock yet.' He remarks that, traditionally, a ghost can
only walk between midnight and dawn, and compares the scene to
Hamlet.[12] But we are dealing with supernatural vengeance, not with a
human ghost urging human revenge. I am not persuaded that the 1826
libretto is not simply an error of literal translation which the old man
never noticed or cared too little about to remedy; it seems improbable,
in any case, that Giovanni would expect to find many unescorted *ragazze*
to hunt in the small hours, that he would have supper at the time sug-

gested (4 a.m.), or that the others should arrive at his house at so bizarre an hour for the *scena ultima*. Equally it will not do to have the invitation and the supper on different nights, following the Benn theory, which ignores the fact that Giovanni and Leporello set off to prepare the meal ('a preperarla andiamo', No. 22). The likelihood is that 'due della notte' means two hours from sunset, which fits with Leporello's claim to an alibi for the beating of Masetto ('I've walked this lady about for an hour or so', II.9) and his appearance at the graveyard, after escaping. If Giovanni looks at a clock or watch he might still translate what he reads into the argot of 'due della notte'; there is thus no difficulty about considering the action as taking place within twenty-four hours.

The two authentic versions of *Don Giovanni*

It is not usual to grant the accolade of authenticity to the Vienna form of *Don Giovanni*. For most critics who have troubled to consider the question, the Vienna version is the first departure from the only true version, that of Prague – even the first betrayal. There is much to be said for this point of view. Nevertheless the Vienna version is unquestionably the work of da Ponte and Mozart, and thus authentic, a statement which need imply neither approval nor disapproval of the changes which distinguish it from the Prague version, nor, in so far as it can be inferred, of their motivation.

One possible area of doubt aside, the facts are clear. The Vienna alterations consisted of (1) the substitution for 'Il mio tesoro' of an aria ('Dalla sua pace' No. 10a) suited to the Vienna tenor, Morella; (2) the insertion of a scene for the Elvira, Cavalieri ('In quali eccessi' – 'Mi tradì' No. 21b); and (3) the insertion of the *buffo* duet ('Per queste tue manine' No. 21a). The last two were embedded in new secco recitatives, and Leporello's escape-aria (No. 20) was omitted. The motivation of (1) is obvious. Morella was not the man for the coloratura aria given to Baglioni; therefore Mozart fitted him out with another piece of similar sentiment and quite different kinds of musical difficulty. The motivation for (2) is a dramatically less justifiable yielding to a singer's demands, for the role was not correspondingly cut. Mozart may have seized upon this chance to fulfil his prescription for equal roles, one *seria* and one of *mezzo carattere* (see above, p. 5), by thus equalizing their solo work as well as their dramatic importance; this aria, however, with its accompanied recitative, brings Elvira temporarily within the *seria* class. All these alterations affect the sensitive point after the sextet, where the original sequence seems least organic. It was obviously the decision to add the duet, and to have the Elvira scena late in the opera because she already has two shorter arias in Act I, that forced the displacement of the tenor aria to Act I.

Don Giovanni has more full arias than *Figaro*, and correspondingly fewer duets, which may be considered a retrograde step. *Figaro* has fourteen arias, actually one more than *Don Giovanni*; but they include the minute one for Barberina and a stage-song for Cherubino, while one of the remaining twelve is a finale ('Non più andrai'). In *Don Giovanni* there is one stage-song (No. 16), and twelve other arias. But *Figaro* in practice is usually cut by omitting the arias of Basilio and Marcellina, justifiably enough since major statements by minor characters are out of place when everything is tending to a conclusion; whereas Ottavio has to have an aria, however dramatically otiose. Otherwise the Prague version deploys its arias well. The only soliloquy (No. 3) is turned into a trio, so that No. 4 is the first really actionless piece, one indispensable as evidence of Giovanni's habits (and incidentally revealing of the character of Leporello and their relationship). Nos. 6 and 8 are as much part of the action as the intervening duet, and the first wholly individual utterance which is also an unadulterated aria is Anna's 'Or sai chi l'onore'; for that reason it would be an effective end to an act, in a placement much favoured by Gluck. The other arias in the original Act I are the short 'Fin ch'an dal vino' and 'Batti, batti'; 'Dalla sua pace' only renders this slight slowing of the action rather more marked. Act II, however, as well as action-arias for Giovanni and Leporello (Nos. 17 and 20), has three long pieces (Nos. 18, 21, and 23) of which it may be said that they no more further the characterization than the action (see below, p. 102, on No. 23, however). The displacement of No. 21 by No. 21b in Vienna merely replaces a virtual with an actual soliloquy. The wish to include both was at one time fulfilled by the desperate remedy of replacing the short recitative after No. 4 by No. 21b, hopelessly inappropriate in this context, and cramming Elvira's three arias into seven consecutive numbers. Properly, however, the Vienna version has one more aria and one more duet than that of Prague.

The problem all producers of *Don Giovanni* face is to maintain the flow of action in the later stages of Act II without sacrificing great dramatic music, a term hardly applicable to the arias usually cut in Act IV of *Figaro*. Although it was composed for a new singer, 'In quali eccessi' explores feelings in keeping with the Prague (and Molière) conception of Elvira (see below, p. 101). But to insert it, as is usually done, after 'Il mio tesoro', results in a sequence of grand arias, with only the short graveyard scene intervening before a third, No. 23; this leads to obvious theatrical embarrassment, hardly mitigated by the expedient of yet another superfluous scene-change for No. 21b, to show Elvira brooding in her hotel. It would therefore be preferable, although not authentic, to replace 'Il mio tesoro' by No. 21b, so that the amount of aria is the same as in the Prague version and Elvira's outburst may seem to be motivated by her humiliation during the sextet, where she pleaded for the life of her *marito* only to find that she had been led about the streets by Leporello. Ottavio would be consoled with No. 10a, the exquisite 'Dalla sua pace', which as it has no *ritornelli* and extravagant coloratura seems more in character than the elaborate 'Il mio tesoro'. The cries of vengeance in the latter are unrelated to Ottavio's temperament and actions, and come too late to change our view of him, whereas 'Dalla sua pace' can establish him as sympathetic, gentle, and affectionate, if ineffectual. It is appropriate for Anna to have two serious arias; she is a vivid, emotional antagonist to Giovanni, and she is the representative of her father whose death indirectly brings about his downfall. Otherwise most of the arias in *Don Giovanni* are as much action-pieces as the ensembles.

The duet No. 21a is the only piece in *Don Giovanni* which does not merit strenuous efforts for its inclusion, and it should only be done if the whole Vienna sequence is undertaken. It is there to remedy the lack of farce, of which there is actually more in *Figaro*; even the Countess' role is *mezzo carattere* and she freely partakes in intrigues to which Anna's masked visit to Giovanni's house is not comparable. The comic bass (Masetto) is more serious than Bartolo, since his aim is not to get rid of a discarded mistress, but to keep a fiancée whom he loves; and da Ponte accordingly endowed him with irony, and postponed the farce of his beating until the second act. There is also more grave and impassioned music in *Don Giovanni*. The duet which places Leporello and Zerlina in a much more crudely comic light is embedded in a sequence of recitative scenes, numbered in the synopsis 10–10d; and Scene 10c includes the revelation of a new crime which motivates 'In quali eccessi' as well as linking up to Giovanni's cheerful escape over the wall of the graveyard.

As only the Neue Mozart Ausgabe includes all the recitatives, some of which were only rediscovered quite recently, it seems worth risking some duplication of the synopsis to show the sequence of the Vienna version (see Table 2).[13]

After the sextet Leporello has no aria but instead continues in recitative, making incoherent apologies to Ottavio until he finds himself by the door and slips out. Masetto and Zerlina pursue him and Ottavio

Table 2. *Sequence of the Vienna version*

		Page in Neue Mozart Ausgabe
I	SEXTET NO. 19 [E♭]	309
II	Scene 9 (recit.) Ottavio: 'Dunque quello sei tu'	350
III	(recit. in lieu of No. 20) Leporello: 'Ah, pietà, compassion, misericordia'	493
IV	Scene 10 (recit.) Elvira: 'Ferma, perfido' (OR beginning: Ottavio: 'Donna Elvira [for 'Amici miei'], dopo eccessi si enormi')	357
V	Scene 10a (recit.) Zerlina: 'Restati quà'	495
VI	DUET No. 21a [C] 'Per queste tue manine'	497
VII	Scene 10b (recit.) Leporello: 'Amico, per pietà, un poco d'acqua fresca' (OR beginning at bar 4: 'Guarda un po' come stretto mi legò l'assassina!')	509
VIII	Scene 10c (recit.) Zerlina: 'Andiam, andiam, signora'	510
IX	Scene 10d Scena No. 21b [E♭] 'In quali eccessi' – 'Mi tradì'	511
X	Scene 11	367
	Alternative recitative within Scene 11	524

addresses his speech to Elvira, then leaves without an aria. It is perfectly plausible that Leporello should be caught by Zerlina in this time and that he should fail to free himself, since he lacks Giovanni's ruthlessness. Newman argues that

No doubt when [this scene] was spatchcocked into the opera . . . a change of scene was made here, regardless of the pre- and post-context. Nobody seems to have reflected then on the absurdity of the peasant girl's making free of the great lady Donna Anna's house in this fashion. The great thing for the groundlings would be Leporello's comic exit with the chair and the window-frame trailing behind him; and for these stage properties a room was of course necessary.[14]

There is, however, no time for the change of set if the musical continuity is to be effective, since Zerlina enters using the music to which Leporello escaped. The 'atrio terreno' of Anna's house, which could be translated 'porch' but must, for the sextet, be a larger enclosed place than that implies, might well have an open window overlooking it, and a chair beneath for sitting outside in. The only question about the continuity is musical. The Neue Mozart Ausgabe editors point out that, since Leporello ran away to the phrase from the omitted No. 20 and Zerlina hauls him back to the same phrase, these two scenes (end of Scene 9 and start of Scene 10a) are consecutive: 'This logical connection of scenes, composed with evident wit, would be sensibly disturbed by the interpolation of Scene 10'.[15] Scene 10, however, contains

Ottavio's momentous pronouncement about going to the police; and is not the reference back to Leporello's escape actually wittier if there is a small intervention (fourteen bars of recitative)? The difficulty is not of dramatic continuity, but of harmony. Ottavio ends his recitative ('così vuole dover, pietade, affetto') in B flat, the key of the omitted No. 21, and Zerlina returns as the continuo outlines a chord of D. Even so the harmonic sequence is not impossible and it is certainly not a sufficient reason for denying the Vienna sequence the cachet of authenticity.

In sum, the Vienna version is one number longer, and has more recitatives. This increase was probably compensated for by cuts in the second finale, perhaps of the entire *scena ultima,* and of literal repetitions in the first finale and the sextet, indicated in the autograph (see below, Chapter 2, n.4). From this the Neue Mozart Ausgabe editors deduce, reasonably enough, that the Vienna version has an experimental and variable form; but that the Prague version alone is an authentic text is a conclusion which goes a little far in the interests of purity. The Vienna version is certainly not, overall, an improvement, despite the beauties of the two new arias. Yet there is no obvious musical and dramatic disfigurement like the arias substituted in the role of Susanna for the 1789 revival of *Figaro*, which are a grotesque sacrifice to the flexible throat of da Ponte's ghastly mistress, La Ferrarese (the first Fiordiligi). Unfortunately we do not know which form of *Don Giovanni* Mozart preferred, although it was probably the original version that he directed, the last time he heard it, in Prague on 2 September 1791, four days before the première of *La clemenza di Tito*. This lack of clear direction from the composer is no excuse today; we should perform either Prague or Vienna entire. But what is normally done is Prague with Nos. 10a and 21b slotted in defiance of authenticity and sense. The reason is that they, and No. 21 which remains, are too beautiful to sacrifice; but if musical beauty is our sole criterion, we should not blame the producer's problems on da Ponte.

Details of the action and characterization

Certain comings and goings in *Don Giovanni* have always seemed to require elucidation, if not apology. For example, before the quartet, as Newman remarks, Elvira 'breaks in upon them with the remark "Ah! do I find you again, perfidious monster?" – which, considering she had left him in that very place only a minute before, can hardly be regarded as a masterpiece of dramatic construction on da Ponte's part'.[16] Almost any dramatic production is liable to fall short of complete plausibility

in such matters, *Figaro* not excepted. But in *Figaro* the location is always clear, and there is only one scene per act, so that designers and
producers are not tempted to folly. In *Don Giovanni*, so long as da
Ponte's directions are adhered to, the action unrolls about as rationally
as the subject-matter allows. Elvira's sudden about-turn is good comedy,
as is the remarkable patience with which she listens to Leporello's in-
credible catalogue (No. 4, allegro) and increasingly lewd description of
its contents (andante). It would be tempting to have her sweep off in
disgust, leaving Leporello, fully in keeping with the traditions to which
he belongs, to sing the andante directly to the audience; but Elvira has
a recitative after No. 4, full of fighting words, and it would be no better
to have her pop in and out like a cuckoo-clock, than to have her take a
prurient interest in Leporello's arithmetic. During Scenes 7-9 she could
go to her lodging and change out of travelling clothes (which she quite
possibly wears to make her entry seem a little ridiculous). Her entrances
to accost Zerlina, and then Anna, certainly present a problem on stage;
not because of the comedy, but because they are deadly serious as well.
It is not clear why Elvira leaves the stage at the end of the quartet; some
synopses assert that Giovanni forces her away, but this is neither authentic, nor plausible (since she could obviously rush back). There is
no suggestion of rough action in the music, and Anna's and Ottavio's
words show that she leaves just as she is winning (as does the music: see
below, p. 99). We learn from Leporello (sc. 15) that she soon resumes
her wrecking activities, taking Zerlina with her to Giovanni's house. If
Zerlina were to hover at the back of the stage during the quartet, Elvira
could exit sweeping her away, and leaving the others in confusion.

One question which concerns details of stage action as well as its
comprehension is Giovanni's sexual success, or lack of it. Otto Rank
noted '(though not without surprise) that the action portrays anything
but a successful sexual adventurer'; Jahn, uncharacteristically literal for
his day, considered that 'the cheerful tone which runs through the
whole opera depends chiefly on the repulses with which the hero is ·
continually met on the field of his heroic deeds'; for Newman, 'of all
the Don Juans of literature and the drama that of da Ponte is pro-
fessionally the most futile'.[17] But it is obviously essential that he
should not *appear* futile, that we should believe in his general success
(unless we try to explain the whole series of misadventures as a misunderstanding, like Shaw in his short story 'Don Giovanni Explains').
Giovanni's power is apparent in 'Là ci darem' and, as he complacently
remarks, the trio No. 15; interruptions to his progress by Elvira or
Masetto are not the result of professional ineptitude. Moberly goes so

far as to explain virtually every absence of Giovanni from the stage by some new conquest, and claims merely to be revealing what is inherent in the opera if properly understood: 'We are accustomed to crime detection in prose. This is sin detection; with all the major clues in the music, and plenty of others in the Italian.' Moberly claims the conquest of Anna, Zerlina, Elvira's maid, and various extras. It is difficult to see why he troubles to make this demonstration since hardly any of it can be shown on the stage, even if one accepts his 'evidence'; and his interpretation seems to be at variance with the authors' intentions.[18] Censorship can hardly have been the problem. Da Ponte not only eschewed what Jahn calls 'the murders and low crimes which were heaped up in the German burlesques of Don Juan',[19] but he carefully removed Bertati's clear indications of 'conquest': Giovanni emerging with Ximena from her house, and shortly afterwards entering Maturina's house with her hand in hand. He is not interrupted; and 'voi sapete quel che fà'. The offensive matter avoided in adapting *Figaro* was political; its sexual implications are all the more marked, and the Count's failure to achieve his end scarcely renders the work more fit for delicate sensibilities.

Does it, in any case, really matter? Giovanni's temporary lack of success (of which he complains, I.11) in his cat-and-mouse game with women does not affect our essential understanding of him as, in Singer's words, 'a professional athlete with a very high batting average ... That he encounters frustrations within the opera simply shows how difficult the sport is.'[20] Da Ponte's handling of the action in this way enriches the characterization, especially of the peasant couple, and makes it more truly comic – for when Elvira bursts in, is it she at whom we laugh, or Giovanni? – and more serious, for all Leporello's list and leer ('and Donn'Anna, did she get what she wanted?').

Anna's seduction or successful resistance is the first and for some the most burning question of the libretto. We are told only what she tells us herself; there was thus a narrow opening for Hoffmann to proclaim that 'the deed was done', and he based his influential interpretation on that 'fact' (see below, p. 130). Einstein, who in his admirable Eulenburg edition of the score claimed to be presenting the work 'in all its clarity, free from all romantic and unromantic obscurities from the 19th century which began as early as E.T.A. Hoffmann', also considered that Anna was seduced:

In the eighteenth century no-one misunderstood this. It goes without saying that in the famous *recitativo accompagnato* [No. 10]...she cannot tell Don Ottavio the whole truth; and his 'respiro' has always had a tragi-comic flavour for every understanding listener. This explains every-thing; Don Giovanni's indifference to her, since he has possessed her just as he has Donna Elvira; her insistence that Don Ottavio must avenge her . . . her refusal to become his, although she loves him; and in the Finale . . . her putting off of Ottavio for another year.[21]

But it explains nothing. For a proud and sensitive girl the attempted outrage upon herself and the consequent murder of her father are suf-ficient cause to insist on revenge; she does not have to have been forcibly, let alone willingly, seduced, to feel guilt at his death. Far from desiring futile heroics from Ottavio, she expresses fear for his safety as they approach Giovanni's house, masked: 'Il passo è periglioso, può nascer qualche imbroglio; temo pel caro sposo e per noi temo ancor.' ('This action is dangerous and may lead to trouble; I fear for my dear betrothed and for us all.') She raises no objection when Ottavio goes to the authorities, and gives no sign that she regards his actions as less than adequate. Her call to revenge, 'Vendetta ti chiedo' (No. 10), does not insist that vengeance take the form of personal combat. The libretto and music make it clear that she loves him – a point on which Einstein diverges from Hoffmann. But she does not refuse him; she insists only on a decent period of mourning. As for Giovanni's alleged indifference, he has few opportunities to show it, let alone to renew his attempt on her, but he certainly responds glowingly enough when she asks for help (I.11), and some significance might be read, at the unmasking, into his addressing Ottavio and Elvira by name, but appealing to Anna: 'Ah, credete . . .'.

Interpretation of Anna is a musical matter (see below, p. 102). With Ottavio we are on more literary ground. He is fated to arrive late, in the first act as in the second finale. Nevertheless he does not merit the usual vilification, some of which stems from Hoffmann's *idée fixe* about Anna:

Torches. Anna and Ottavio enter: a dressy little coxcomb of no more than twenty-one. As Anna's fiancé he apparently lives in the house, since he has been summoned so quickly; at the first alarm, which he must have heard, he could have hurried and saved her father; he had to dress first, and doesn't much like going out at night.[22]

The explanation of his presence may lie in da Ponte's sources. In Bertati Giovanni mocks Anna, saying 'Se fosse il Duca Ottavio nemmeno parlereste' ('If I were Duke Ottavio you would not talk like that' – i.e. call him traitor and a man without honour). She replies that the Duke would never act so basely. Da Ponte's concern for speed of action led him to suppress this laborious exchange. The idea goes back to Tirso, who has Juan twice deceive a lover by anticipating a rendezvous in the dark (see above, p. 37). From Tirso, too, comes the idea of Anna as the crucial failure from which Giovanni's downfall springs. Nevertheless da Ponte may have expected us to understand what Bertati implies, that Anna was prepared for a nocturnal visit from Ottavio; she herself says that she first took the stranger for him. This interpretation at least absolves us from Peter Hall's expedient of having him arrive in his nightshirt. (Although Hall's idea of an older, paternal Ottavio is sympathetic and effective, it is not necessary to establishing an affectionate relationship between the couple.)

Ottavio's behaviour, throughout, is exemplary. He does everything the situation demands; he keeps his head. We need not infer from this any indifference to Anna's suffering, and the music tells us of his tender, agonized concern in a few bars of andante (No. 2, bars 48-50). After Anna's revelation he seeks for evidence, entering Giovanni's house masked; he draws a pistol, in defence of Leporello, but he should put it away after unmasking, for its purpose is served. Da Ponte does not suggest that he betrays any hostile intention by carrying a sword to the dance (a point overlooked by producers since Hoffmann's time). He could not assassinate Giovanni in his own house, for that would be to answer crime with crime.[23] He is perfectly prepared to kill him during the sextet, for then 'Giovanni' is trespassing on Anna's property, late at night, and summary justice is in order. On finding that it is Leporello he decides to invoke civil authority. For once, misunderstanding of this admirable character is not resisted by the music. Practical virtues do not make arias; expressions of revenge belong to Elvira and Anna; Ottavio's solos are of melting tenderness, and lack the heroic ring.

The first finale

The Prague libretto of 1787 contains a number of stage-directions which are not normally all reproduced, but which alone make perfect sense of the dance-scene and its sequel. Some were already missing from the 1788 (Vienna) libretto, although nothing replaced them:

Bar

437 Giovanni begins to dance with Zerlina (Contredanse).

453 Leporello makes Masetto dance (Teitsch).

456 Giovanni: 'Vieni con me . . .' Dancing, he leads Zerlina to a door and makes her go through as if by force. Masetto: 'Ah nò! Zerlina!' Breaks free of Leporello and follows Zerlina.

460 Leporello: 'Qui nasce una ruina.' Goes off in a hurry.

467 Zerlina: 'Gente, aiuto . . .' From without; struggle (*strepito*) from the right.

474 Masetto: 'Ah Zerlina.' From without. The musicians and the others leave in confusion.
476 The scream and struggle are heard from the opposite side.
486 Maskers: 'Ah gittiamo giù la porta.' Breaking down the door. Zerlina: 'Soccoretimi.' Comes in from another direction.
499 [Giovanni] Comes in sword in hand. With him he leads Leporello by the arm and pretends to purpose stabbing him; but the sword does not leave the sheath.

How is all this to be understood? Giovanni has to use some force to remove Zerlina, which entails an unwanted risk; no doubt he believes her willing. Certainly she takes a risk with him, for she is high-spirited and irked by Masetto's jealousy. If the staging can suggest three rooms in which the three dances take place, Giovanni may plausibly not notice how his plan to decoy Masetto is failing.[24]

Giovanni's threat to kill Leporello may seem a ridiculous piece of play-acting, and it is perhaps a legitimate distortion to have his sword drawn as if to stab in earnest. But this trick is improvised for an audience of gullible peasantry and hired musicians (it is a bad mistake to have any guests of higher class, other than the maskers, in this scene). When he finds nobody left but his victim, Masetto, and the three who now unmask, he is human enough to be staggered. In the allegro he and Leporello at first express only confusion. The others threaten to proclaim his villainy to the world: 'Hear the thunder of revenge. . .its bolt shall fall on your head this very day.' As is customary at the end of a finale, the action freezes; most of the characters dissolve their identities into a chorus (the nineteenth century saw this as an opportunity actually to use the chorus, having failed to send off the extras at bar 474).

Giovanni's enemies are momentarily inspired by prophecy, but he is in no immediate danger from any of them. Nor is there any supernatural warning. Many commentators speak confidently of actual thunder at this point, and productions since Hoffmann have introduced it. Dent, however, rightly protested

against the thunder and lightning which invariably accompany the last movement. This is based on a misunderstanding of da Ponte's words. He gives no indication of a storm in his stage directions, which are numerous and fairly complete; and it is quite clear that the storm with its thunder and lightning alluded to in the words actually sung is to be construed in a purely metaphorical sense.[25]

Mozart confirms this judgment by a profusion of drum-rolls which render superfluous any assistance from other sound-effects (not to mention electric light). It is not a musical representation of a storm;

rather it suggests confusion and anger. It is true that human rage is impotent against Giovanni; but that is all the more reason for avoiding supernatural excesses, which would, moreover, undermine the climax of Act II.

So what does happen? Properly speaking, nothing. The usual action is described by Hoffmann: Giovanni 'smites the bridegroom's trumpery sword from his hand and makes his way through the profane rabble, who all comically fall over each other, opening a way to freedom like bold Roland thrusting through the army of the tyrant Cymork.' Even in Jahn's sober synopsis Giovanni 'boldly and irresistibly makes his way through his enemies'. These antics resulted from the degeneration in performing style which set in in Germany even before Mozart's death. Dent described a producer's whim whereby 'Elvira in a sudden fit of passion throws herself in front of Giovanni to cover his escape'; in one modern libretto Giovanni 'seizes Leporello, and pushing the servant before himself, forces his way through the crowd which surrounds him and escapes'.[26] But the 'crowd' is five people, three of them women; Masetto is unarmed; Ottavio has a pistol but excellent reasons not to use it (see above). The scene is not a duel; it is not the confrontation of a criminal with the forces of law, or with divine justice; it is a social contretemps. And it is an operatic finale; the faster the music, the slower the action, as we move into what Hall has well called 'suspended time'. The Act II finale of *Figaro* is certainly the model, although it contains no question of bloodshed and the plot has reached a point of utmost complication. In *Don Giovanni* the plot has suddenly simplified; the battle-lines are drawn, the avengers unmasked. But the union of antagonists at this moment is artificial, and their pursuit of Giovanni in Act II initially follows independent lines. Giovanni has admitted nothing and he remains in command of his destiny, at least in society. He would doubtless have made some spectacular escape had the police appeared with Ottavio later on; here there is no need. His courage revives; the music suggests that he stands, full of effrontery, and brazens it out. There is no reason to suppose that Mozart or da Ponte conceived the lack of action at the end of a finale as a problem, or indeed that they gave it a moment's thought.

Act II

I have suggested that the structure of Act II may abide our question. Nevertheless, apart from the troublesome sequence after the sextet, it contains hardly any problematical details, and is perfectly coherent on its own level. One may wonder why, during the coda to No. 17, Giovanni takes Masetto off and then leads him back in order to beat him. Moberly suggests that in fact he takes him elsewhere, out of sight, for the beating, and then returns to Elvira's maid.[27] This is ingenious and plausible; and with a little good-will from the audience it can be staged. One conquest Giovanni may well be allowed, albeit disguised as Leporello.

At the start of the finale Giovanni is often seen surrounded by company, mainly female; we learn from Hoffmann that this too is an early tradition. It seems unlikely that, as is sometimes asserted, these whores who often grace the supper were Mozart's idea (still less the cavaliers who are sometimes permitted to share them). Whores, requiring no seduction-game, are superfluous to Giovanni, and unlike the mute servants who are an integral part of the scene they detract from the comic business and from the vivid pathos of Elvira's entrance.[28] The only extras required in *Don Giovanni* are the peasants and servants who sing in Act I; the demons are invisible, although here too a tradition quickly became established of bringing them on stage, as in Bertati, particularly when the *scena ultima* was suppressed.

The problem of the *scena ultima* is one of convention. The characters assume two roles, their own and that of a chorus, as in the first finale. Anna enters with a grotesque lapse into the *buffo* genre to which she does not belong, with words more suited to the Zerlina of the Vienna duet No. 21a: 'Solo mirandolo stretto in catene alle mie piene calma darò' ('My anguish will only be soothed by seeing him tightly bound in chains').[29] The characters react chorally to Leporello's narrative but revert to type with the larghetto; Ottavio and Anna have *opera seria* warblings of regret, Elvira speaks briefly, the others have lines of *buffo* character. It is the three plebeians who go into chorus ('Resti dunque quel birbon'), the others following at the fugue. The Epilogue to *The Rake's Progress* clearly owes much to this *scena ultima;* but Auden and Stravinsky, whose characters remove their wigs and sing with the houselights on, were playing with a convention which they understood historically. It is far less clear in *Don Giovanni* at what point the actors shed their assumed identities and speak as actors. We may be thankful that da Ponte rejected the idiotic finale of Bertati, in which they all, irrespective of class, dance and mimic musical instruments.

There is a final hollowness at the end of several of Mozart's great operas, but if it is a flaw it is one which arises only through their supreme quality. In *Don Giovanni* and to a lesser extent *Così* the vacuum is filled by lively speculation about the characters' destinies, but such intellectual games cannot repair a damaged work. In *Figaro* there is true reconciliation, and that nobody can believe in its durability hardly affects the integrity of the work. In *Die Zauberflöte* good easily overcomes the last foray of evil before the glowing finale. In *Don Giovanni* there is reconciliation for two pairs of lovers; and evil is overcome. Unfortunately a modern audience (and in such matters audiences became modern with Romanticism) is likely to find the classical rounding-off too neat, a trivialization of the action. The visit of the stone guest has some connection with the classical *deus ex machina,* and a final scene, with its necessary concluding emphasis on the main key, may be seen as an element of musical language corresponding to this feature of neo-classical drama; hence the happy endings of Gluck's neo-classical reform operas, and of *Idomeneo.* But this convention sits uncomfortably beside those of *opera buffa.* It is too easy to explain such incongruities, such problematic endings, as 'ambiguous'; what gives rise to doubt in the case of *Don Giovanni* is not ambiguity in itself, but the authors' unawareness of it, their apparent belief that everything has been resolved.

5 'Don Giovanni' in the theatre

Don Giovanni is an indispensable part of the repertory of any opera company; the main roles, and the opera as a whole, have an irresistible and sometimes fatal attractiveness for singers, designers, producers, conductors. Few have heeded Bernard Shaw's plaintive question: 'Why not leave Don Giovanni in peace on the shelf? It is so easy not to perform it.'[1] Of course *Don Giovanni* belongs in the theatre; yet most thoughtful opera-goers would probably agree that there can be no completely satisfying version, as there can be of *Figaro* or *Cosi*. And in performance, as Noske remarks with a proper indignation, 'indisputable facts and even da Ponte's simple but very efficient stage directions are disregarded again and again. Not only local but also international festival performances suffer from this treatment. Obviously the opera has become an object solely for the private pleasure of stage directors and conductors.'[2]

Productions to 1800

Because reviewing of theatrical productions was not permitted in Joseph II's Austria, we really know very little about the performances directed by Mozart except that he was happy, at least, about the Prague ones.[3] The enduring affection of that city for *Don Giovanni* is attested by writers of the early nineteenth century such as Mozart's biographers, Niemetschek and Nissen, and Stiepanek, who in 1825 made the first Czech version; by that date it had had over a hundred performances in Italian and twice as many in German. The first production was not given by a star cast but by a company which, accustomed to Mozart by *Figaro,* played as a team. The excellence of the orchestra may be taken for granted, and there is little doubt that by 29 October 1787 a brilliant performance had been put together. Here is the cast, with their roles in *Figaro,* where known, appended: Giovanni, Luigi Bassi (the Count); Ottavio, Antonio Baglioni; Leporello, Felice Ponziani (Figaro); Commendatore/Masetto, Giuseppe Lolli; Anna, Teresa Saporiti; Elvira, Caterina Micelli; Zerlina, Caterina Bondini, wife of the impresario (Susanna). Mozart knew all the singers except Baglioni, who at the time of the Prague *Figaro* was singing the title-role in Gazzaniga's *Don Giovanni* in Venice, and his knowledge of them is reflected in the composition.[4] Bassi, a remarkable artist of only twenty-two, as is fitting for a *giovane cavalier*, had a gift for mimicry, Ponziani for patter. Silhouettes of the singers commemorate the occasion, and a contemporary illustration shows Bassi serenading, but no other pictorial record of the scenery survives.[5] The theatre was equipped to alternate half- and full-stage sets within each act (see above, Chapter 2); probably, like da Ponte's stage-directions, its style was simple but efficient. Bitter concludes that the production was characterized by moderation and subtlety, avoiding extremes of passion and buffoonery (despite the penchant for improvisation; see above, p. 3).[6] Guardasoni took the company to Leipzig in June 1788, but with Kosta for Bassi, Crespi for Saporiti, and another Micelli for Bondini; and to Warsaw in October 1789, although a *Don Giovanni* by Albertini had received its première there only six years before.

The cast in Vienna in 1788 was rather different from that which had introduced *Figaro* almost exactly two years earlier: Giovanni, Francesco Albertarelli; Ottavio, Francesco Morella; Leporello, Francesco Benucci (Figaro); Commendatore/Masetto, Francesco Bussani (Bartolo/Antonio); Anna, Aloysia Lange; Elvira, Caterina Cavalieri; Zerlina, Luisa Mombelli (Countess). Mombelli was the company's *prima donna;* she was given Zerlina because of pregnancy, and during the summer she resigned the role to Therese Teyber. Cavalieri had been Constanze in *Die Entführung;* Mozart had already made sacrifices to her 'flexible throat' (letter of 26 September 1781), and she was obviously suited to Elvira's flighty style. Accordingly her new aria, 'Mi tradì', conforms well with the rest of the role. Lange was Mozart's sister-in-law and first love. She received no new aria, but was consoled by a concert aria, 'Ah, se in ciel, benigne stelle' K.539, written in March. Albertarelli and Morella were new members of the company; the latter received 'Dalla sua pace', the former an arietta for insertion into an opera by Anfossi (K.541), composed in May. Mombelli and Benucci, the latter a favourite of Mozart's and an excellent buffoon, received the duet 'Per queste tue manine'. *Don Giovanni* was given twelve times between 7 May and 2 August, and thrice more in October, November, and December. On 24 May extracts of the music were offered for sale (manuscript copies, not including numbers omitted in the Vienna version).[7] It is clear that the work was less well received in Vienna, and it was not *Don Giovanni* but the successful revival of *Figaro* in 1789 which led to the commission for the last Mozart–da Ponte opera, *Così fan tutte*. Again, however, information is scanty. From the tradition of Viennese theatre and the type of alteration made, it is apparent that there was already a divergence between the increasingly coarse comedy and the serious aspects, so that the precarious harmony of the original conception was already damaged under the eyes of Mozart and da Ponte themselves.

The authentic versions of *Don Giovanni* travelled slowly, and have actually had to be revived, since knowledge of them was positively obstructed, especially in Germany, by the rapid diffusion of versions which preserved Mozart's music but supplanted da Ponte with texts belonging to quite different theatrical traditions. It became *Don Juan,* subtitled *'ein Singspiel'* (a German-language opera with spoken dialogue; no German text was fitted to Mozart's recitatives until 1845).[8] There were productions in some sixteen German cities before Mozart's death, in seven different translations. The first German text was by Beethoven's teacher C. G. Neefe, used at Mannheim and Bonn in September and October 1789.[9] The first translation actually performed was that of H. G. Schmieder, by the Mainz company at Mainz and Frankfurt in March and May 1789; and *Don Juan* appeared that year at Passau, Hamburg, Graz, and Brno. A translation by F. L. Schröder was used at Hamburg, and at Berlin (December 1790); it already divides the work into four acts. In 1791 major centres reached include Hanover, Kassel, Munich, Cologne, and possibly Prague itself; but unless Mozart saw a reputed performance at the Prague Vaterländisches Theater im Hiberner Kloster, neither he nor da Ponte witnessed any of these travesties. Whereas a *Singspiel* version of *Figaro* could hardly depart far from Beaumarchais, *Don Giovanni* fell all too readily into vulgar traditions, a fact to which its rapid growth in popularity throughout Germany may be attributed; only *Die Zauberflöte* travelled faster, and it was a *Singspiel* from the start. The first published German translation, by Friedrich Rochlitz (1801), remained in use for half a century; it drew freely on its predecessors, so that ideas originating with Neefe or Schröder became accepted as part of Mozart's opera, and Freisauff, writing as late as 1887, still had to explain that several features were not originally part of the opera at all.[10]

These versions were influenced by the German popular or subliterary tradition, which had had no impact on da Ponte. The puppet-plays mingled moralizing with low farce and violence, and gave prominence to the servant (Hanswurst). The authentic Vienna version had pointed this way; but while early translators avoided obscenities in the text, the performers put them back, causing the Munich censor to ban the piece for a while. More surprising is a renewed influence of Molière. Neefe's intentions are apparent from his title: *Der bestrafte Wüstling oder Der Krug geht so lange zu Wasser bis er bricht*: *Il dissoluto punito*, or *The Pitcher Goes to the Well until It Breaks,* Molière's moralizing line for Sganarelle as he reproaches Juan for hypocrisy. Giovanni is named Schwänkenreich; Marianne (Anna) has for fiancé Fischblut (fishblood), in which Neefe declares himself the first critic of poor Ottavio. Leporello is Fickfack, the peasants Gürge and Röschen, but for some reason there remains 'Elvire aus Burgos', casting some doubt on the location. These names were in practice rejected in favour of the originals, with the Commendatore having his traditional name of Pedro; sometimes Ottavio was Gussman, a misplaced reminiscence of Elvire's servant in Molière.

Elvira was the main victim of these manipulations. The four-act form concentrated in the first act on Anna, in the second on Zerlina. The third ended with 'Il mio tesoro' so that the fourth began in the grave-yard. The *scena ultima,* whose survival in Vienna in 1788 is in doubt (see below, Chapter 2, n. 4), perished miserably in a flood of brimstone, and the statue abetted the demons, becoming an instrument of ven-geance rather than warning – a misunderstanding common today. These changes were made even in versions in Italian, with recitatives; but the *Singspiel* form readily permitted the inclusion of additional dialogue scenes which still further unbalanced the dramatic and musical struc-ture. Neefe included a scene from Molière in which Juan outwits a creditor (M. Dimanche), and a scene with a minister of justice, perhaps inspired by Juan's father in Molière. The amoral, almost spiritual Giovanni of Mozart becomes a cad and swindler. Yet Stiepanek retained these scenes in his Czech translation 'because the character of Don Juan is so much illuminated by them'. Schröder added a grotesque episode in the graveyard, possibly derived from *L'ateista fulminato* by way of the puppet theatre. Juan, actively pursued by Oktavio, manages to exchange cloaks with a hermit. Thus disguised he persuades Oktavio that it is impious not to rely on divine vengeance; when he flings down his weapons, Juan murders him.[11] Naturally there could be no *scena ultima* in this version, and Act II Scene 12 necessarily became a solil-oquy. This last idea had a long currency. Ottavio's words are read by Anna from a letter; 'Non mi dir' is sometimes referred to as the 'letter-aria'.

It is not surprising that critics noticed the discrepancy, so nearly

resolved in the original version, between the callous brutality of the action and the beauty of the music. Typical is a report from Berlin in the Weimar *Journal des Luxus und der Moden* (February 1791): 'The music of this Singspiel is beautiful, but here and there very artificial, difficult, and overloaded with instrumental detail. The contents of the play are the old well-known subject, which pleases the general public only because of the burlesque jests of Leporello, whilom Jack Pudding [Hanswurst], and of the stone Commendatore on horseback. . .'[12] The music was caviar to the general, and appealed no more to the middlebrow critic than did the farcical 'play'. But this was Schröder's translation, still further degraded by the Berlin performer in the title-role, Friedrich Lippert, nominally a tenor but more actor than singer, and a ham.

These extra scenes were not always included, and South German performances were more modest. The first Vienna *Singspiel* production, by Schikaneder at the Theater auf der Wieden in 1792 (translation by C. H. Spiess), was reasonably authentic. Regrettably, the next, at the Kärntnerthortheater in 1798, was given by Lippert and conducted by Mozart's pupil Süssmayr.[13] It is regrettable, also, that the first good pictures of scenery come from versions based on Neefe. They are by members of the ubiquitous Quaglio family, two of whom, the brothers Joseph and Julius, had been active in Mannheim since 1770. The Mannheim graveyard (see Fig. 1) is probably by Julius, and since it is clearly designed for an eighteenth-century theatre with side-flats and an elegant baroque perspective, it probably represents a style similar to that used at Prague. Certainly it reflects over a century of operatic tradition. There are skulls a-plenty, but the obelisk consorts with the pure Mediterranean forms of the cypresses, backed by a pedimented gate. Joseph's design for Munich (1791, preserved in a watercolour by Angelo I Quaglio) already introduces Romantic disorder: a mountain, diverse tree and tomb forms, and an equestrian Commendatore (which da Ponte did not specify) on a rearing horse (see Fig. 2).[14]

The nineteenth century

The Romantic interest in the supernatural, and the recognition accorded to Mozart by all Europe in the decade after his death, doubtless saved from extinction the mixture of brutal realism and grotesque supernatural that *Don Giovanni* had become. Translations were made into numerous other languages, and there was international interest in Italian versions. Italy took it up, naturally in the original language, and in some-

thing like an authentic form – mutilated, that is, more gently, by cuts rather than the introduction of alien dramatic elements. It may have been tried out in Florence in 1798; an important score survives there, based directly on the Vienna version.[15] The first performance was in Rome (1811); Stendhal reports that it was found to be over-orchestrated. Italy greeted *Don Giovanni* with more respect than affection at first, and the dance-scene in the Act I finale was a nearly insuperable obstacle. The Italians did not favour the mixture of serious and comic elements, and although the opera was at first subtitled *dramma semiserio*, it was drawn into the ambiance of the Ottocento and called *melodramma giocoso*. Again, Elvira suffered; her mixed nature was not understood, and Nos. 8 and 21b were amputated, making Anna the undisputed *prima donna*, as she was universally regarded throughout the century; even singers who made their mark with Zerlina, such as Adelina Patti, aspired to become Anna.[16] Yet even Anna occasionally lost No. 10, and once 'Non più di fiori' from *La clemenza di Tito* replaced 'Non mi dir'; the libretto pointed out that it was, after all, by Mozart. Other *buffo* elements were removed, including the *scena ultima*, and, as everywhere else, the devils invaded the stage. Naples saw *Don Giovanni* in 1812, Milan in 1814, Florence in 1817. Other cities followed, but its spiritual home, Venice, waited until 1833, by which time an apology was called for; the delay was blamed on problems of casting and, even at this date, on difficult orchestral parts.[17]

In Germany, literature was influenced by *Don Giovanni*, and in turn affected performances, which became Romanticized, sincere, forgetful of *opera buffa*. E. T. A. Hoffmann interpreted the hero's game as a Faustian striving for unattainable perfection in Woman (this would have surprised Leporello: 'He conquers even the old ones, for the pleasure of putting them on the list' (No.4)) (see below, pp. 83 and 128). Giovanni's crimes are justified by this transcendental quest, and the *burlador* becomes sombre, introspective, cousin to other Romantic misfits and outcasts like Hamlet and Schiller's Karl Moor. Against him stands Anna, violated, passionately attracted to the man she must destroy. This interpretation, which mixes Anna's feelings quite unwarrantably, was widely accepted. It seems to have encouraged larger voices, in larger houses – both fashionable in the period – to deliver her music more slowly and heavily. In general, Mozart tempi were tending in this period towards extremes, some of which are still with us. The direction 'Andante ₵' implies a medium speed and does not admit of much variation; thus the opening of the Overture, the quartet, 'Or sai chi l'onore', and the sextet should be roughly equal in tempo. The last two are controlled by rapid enunciation of words; but 'Or sai' is sometimes accelerated, some-times retarded, in the interests of 'interpretation', and the statue music is often slowed to adagio. (Worst of all is the unmusical scramble so often made of 'Fin ch'an dal vino'.)[18]

The first production and revivals of *Don Giovanni* in any particular centre, however illustrious, are important more to the history of that opera house than to the history of Mozart's work. Such histories are re-plete with piquant detail: the gendarmes who sang the masked trio in the first Paris production (see below); the breakdown in the finale of the first American performance, given by Garcia's company under the aegis of the aging da Ponte (New York, 1826); the early Russian perfor-mance (Moscow, 1806) which not only used a tenor Giovanni (as did many performances; it is after all preferable to a bass) but had Ottavio, reverting to *opera seria* type, sung by a soprano. Like Prague, Russia saw *Don Giovanni* in three languages, German, Italian, and Russian (the latter first at St Petersburg, 1828).[19] In London, Italian and English versions were characteristically juxtaposed in 1817 at the Haymarket and Covent Garden; the latter was anglicized as *The Libertine* (Shadwell's title), with music adapted by the inevitable Henry Bishop. As late as 1851, London tolerated Costa's disgraceful amplification of the supper music by an ophicleide solo. As Berlioz, that apostle of authenticity, bitterly remarked, 'was not Don Juan a man of taste?'.[20]

The city in which *Don Giovanni* had its liveliest and most varied existence, outside Germany, was probably Paris. Three main trends of performance style were represented at different theatres: singers' opera, vernacular comic opera, grand opera. The first French performance was the appalling adaptation by Kalkbrenner (1805), with much additional music. The first performance in Italian was under Spontini, in 1811. But its establishment in Paris really dates from the epoch of Roman-ticism, around 1830. The equivalent to Bishop, Castil-Blaze, fitted it out as an *opéra comique* with spoken dialogue (1827, Théâtre de l'Odéon), using Molière – a much sillier idea than the practice, adhered to until recently in Paris, of giving Rossini's *Barber* with Beaumarchais' dialogue. 'The two elements preclude each other', as a critic remarked of a similar attempt in 1866 at the Théâtre Lyrique. The Théâtre des Italiens launched *Don Giovanni* as a singers' opera, with Anna as the prize role (Grisi) among the women; there were also Tamburini, Lablache (who is credited with being the first Leporello to sing the final innuendo of 'Madamina' through his nose) and the matchless Rubini. If Wagner is to be believed, the result was dramatically desultory; the Anna–Gio-vanni relationship (which he understood in Hoffmann's way) was unclear;

the audience was half bored, half expectant: 'In due course the mystery was solved: *Rubini that evening delivered his famous trill on top A and top B flat'* (which will not, of course, be found in any score of 'Il mio tesoro').[21]

The Opéra produced a grand staging of *Don Giovanni* in 1834, with Nourrit, a tenor but a fine singer and thoughtful actor, in the title-role and the admirable Levasseur as Leporello – sombre in jest, even satanic, according to one admiring critic. This was the production reviewed by Berlioz (see below, p. 131), who confirms that the chorus, in keeping with the traditions of this theatre, intervened to end Act I. Ballet was also demanded at the Opéra, and as late as 1900 a score 'conforming to the performances of the Académie Nationale [Opéra]' was published, in five acts, lacking the *scena ultima*, but with additional ballets and entr'actes from Mozart's other works. Almost the only friend of the *scena ultima* in the nineteenth century was that eccentric hangover, from the Age of Reason, Peacock, who called the final fugue 'one of the very finest things in dramatic music, and the most appropriate possible termination for the subject'.[22] One critic vigorously attacked the Théâtre Lyrique for daring to include it: 'The spirit of the master-piece is not enough for them, they want also the letter . . !' As for the Opéra's sets, 'We must thank M. Véron for naturalizing Mozart's master-piece . . . for rejuvenating a first-rate musical drama by such splendid decorations, such sumptuous costumes, without which it would be passable, but from which it can only gain.'[23]

Don Giovanni passed through the fire of Wagnerism, to be granted the sobriquet *Musikdrama* by many; and as late as 1918 Ernst Lert exclaimed: 'Ein Bacchusmythos, eine dionysische Tragödie ist der "Don Giovanni".'[24] Nevertheless, well before the turn of the century, a revival of interest in the original form and ambiance began. The centenary in 1887 aroused considerable interest, and besides numerous celebratory performances, most of them doubtless quite unregenerate, excellent historical studies appeared by Chrysander, Freisauff, and Engel, and in 1892 by Procházka.[25] In 1896 Victor Maurel published a short book about staging *Don Giovanni* in which he points out various common musical misinterpretations and pleads eloquently for smaller orchestras and smaller opera houses, so that the wealth of detail, of which the early critics had complained, and which grandiose perform-ance tended to drown, could make a proper impact. The Giovanni of Maurel, Verdi's first Iago and Falstaff, was evidently a subtle, studied performance; too much so, according to Shaw, who saw it in London in 1891: 'He gave us a description of Don Juan rather than an impersonation of him.'[26] Also in 1896, a production at Munich inaugurated the use of a revolving stage designed by Karl Lautenschläger for the Königliches Residenztheater, said to be the only one operating at that date outside Japan (see Fig. 3). Dent underlined the importance of swift action in this opera; the rapid scene-changing by revolving stage matched that of the eighteenth century's flats. The first tableau of Act I was identified with the second of Act II, and was well provided with gates for Leporello to mistake (see Fig. 4a). The style was by now rather conventionally Romantic, notably in the Gothic, ivy-covered graveyard scene (see Fig. 4b).[27]

The twentieth century

In 1913 Dent, in his book on Mozart's operas which is still the touchstone for such studies, reacted forcefully against Romantic over-inflation of *Don Giovanni*, going almost too far in elimination of what may be called the tragic element. Others, like Lert, owing allegiance to traditions by now a century old, sought to maintain or revive them. There is such diversity of practice that no twentieth-century style of production exists, but instead a vigorous, if often misdirected, eclecticism. We seek for relevance to our time, but self-consciously, whereas earlier periods did so naturally. We seek for authenticity, about which earlier periods cared very little. We seek to reflect psychological and literary commentaries, or even to resuscitate theatrically lively but inauthentic practices.

Probably the main trouble with *Don Giovanni* in the theatre is that it acts so directly and subtly through its music that in truth it needs no staging. The art of the producer must be either to conceal art and faithfully represent the clear intentions of the authors, or to reimagine the work to the extent that we witness not Mozart's and da Ponte's *Don Giovanni*, but a single, distorted, sometimes brilliantly illuminated, view of it. The first attitude would employ the obvious locations for the action, and appropriate costumes, either for sixteenth-century Spain or for eighteenth-century Venice. The second takes such desperate measures as Peter Hall's setting (Glyndebourne, 1977) in the French Empire period. What is unforgivable is only the dramatically inept handling of detail, as for instance in the at times very brilliant, but thoroughly misconceived, production by David Pountney, whose cleverness is unfortunately at war with the work in a manner unmatched even by Hall's wilder imagination. Curiously enough, the production (Scottish Opera, 1979) seems to seek, among other things, to revive a nineteenth-century

3 b   Carl Lautenschläger, mechanism of revolving stage with graveyard; Anna's room; (inset) garden of Commendatore's house (Munich, 1896)

3 a   Carl Lautenschläger, plan of revolving stage (Munich, 1896)

4a Carl Lautenschläger, garden of Commendatore's house (Act I, Tableau 1; Act II, Tableau 2) (Munich, 1896)

4b Carl Lautenschläger, graveyard (Munich, 1896)

splendour in a tradition continuously employed until recently at the Paris Opéra. Numerous meticulously rehearsed extras are kept as busy as possible (friends of Ottavio, servants, peasants, publicans, priests, aristocratic guests unaccountably present in the first finale, etc.). A rather beautiful scene had Ottavio singing 'Dalla sua pace' while Anna knelt in prayer by her father's bier, with a full complement of pall-bearers and clergy. The relation between this young couple was sensitively handled, contrary to the literary influences elsewhere apparent.[28] But there was also much foolishness: Elvira's hooped dress and Anna's prematurely donned mourning, for example, which made them hopelessly recognizable beneath their masks. When in the nineteenth century 'Non mi dir' became a soliloquy, it was often treated as a prayer.[29] Pountney revived this idea, with Anna flinging herself before a prie-dieu, although Ottavio was present, and although the Italian (which was being sung) means 'Perhaps one day Heaven will take pity', indubitably not a prayer-like text.

It is perhaps fortunate that no amount of ingenuity can permit producers to answer the burning question of what actually happened to Anna, although Hall for one evidently pondered it deeply. Staging of the concluding scenes, however, shows signs both of literary influence and of reconsideration of the earliest sources of the story. Thus the mostly sensible and sober production for English National Opera by Anthony Besch (1976; revived 1980) brought the Commendatore to Giovanni's house on horseback, although Leporello's description of his approach − 'Ta ta ta ta' − could not apply to a horse. Giovanni had to make an undignified scramble, thoroughly at odds with the music, to reach the statue's hand. When he was swallowed up by the pedestal, the horse rearing up to allow him entrance, there seemed to be a reference to the second supper in the Commendatore's grave in early versions including Tirso (see above, p. 36). Pountney seems to point still further back, to an alleged origin of the story in which Spanish monks killed the *burlador* and pretended it was divine vengeance, to discourage the others. Priests, left over from the earlier funeral scene, replaced the devils who ought not to appear anyway. This revival of the religious element may have been suggested by Brophy, who calls *Don Giovanni* 'a thoroughgoing Catholic opera'.[30] She hints that Giovanni, being essentially indestructible, and leaving no body, might even be resurrected. Pountney's priests accordingly raised Giovanni as if crucified on his own table; he fell below to be concealed by a flame-coloured cloth, from which he was seen to emerge before the curtain fell. On the table a scorched cloth remained, a relic in which Elvira showed interest during the *scena ultima,* while at the front of the stage the harmless catalogue was solemnly burnt. It is to be hoped that this represents a nadir, but in the light of elegant imbecilities such as Losey's film it is hard to be sanguine. Any producer, conductor, and author, will testify that Shaw was wrong; it is, no doubt, not easy to perform *Don Giovanni,* but neither is it 'so easy not to perform' it, for it simply will not leave one alone.

6 Don Giovanni as an idea [1]

BERNARD WILLIAMS

Giovanni is Don Juan, but he does not have to bear the weight of all the significance which that mythical figure has come to express. Still less does Giovanni have to be pursued, as though by another Elvira, with every interpretation that has been given of Don Juanism as a psychological category: that it expresses latent homosexuality, for instance, or hatred of women, or a need for reassurance. Any of these may be true of the local womanizer, but he is not Giovanni, and these states of mind are not what *Don Giovanni* expresses.

Some later Don Juans, elaborated as they all are with a vast variety of metaphysical, social or psychological reflections, are closer relatives of Giovanni than others. Most remote are the negative, melancholic, or merely frantic embodiments of the hero: fleeing from exhaustion and inner emptiness, in Lenau's representation, or, according to George Sand and Flaubert, engaged in a despairing hunt for a genuine encounter with another person. These, at any rate, are not Giovanni, who is as unambiguously and magnificently removed from despair and boredom as it is possible to be. At the climax of the opera, his words are in praise of women and wine, 'sostegno e gloria d'umanità' ('support and glory of mankind'), but his music encompasses a larger praise of life and humanity themselves.

This chapter is concerned only with Giovanni's closer relatives in the tradition. Moreover, it is interested in them only in so far as they seem to help in thinking about the opera. They are, of course, rarely independent of the opera. Later writers have not simply gone back to some archetype of Don Juan, or taken Mozart's opera merely as one previous embodiment of that character, but have in many cases been quite specially influenced by the opera. Indeed, nineteenth- and twentieth-century thoughts about Don Juan have been dominated by Mozart's embodiment of him. This is not merely because the opera is by far the greatest work given to this theme. It is also because the opera is in various ways problematical, and that it raises in a challenging way the

81

question of what the figure of Giovanni means. Hence, not only is the opera the historical starting-point of many modern thoughts on this subject, but some of those thoughts lead directly back to the problem of understanding the opera itself.

What are we to make of Giovanni? The opera is named after him, it is about him, it is he who holds together a set of scenes in other ways rather disconnected. He is in a deep way the life of the opera, yet the peculiarity is that such character as he has is not really as grand as that implies: he expresses more than he is. He seems to have no depth adequate to the work in which he plays the central role. He has, in a sense, a character – to a considerable extent a bad one. But we are not given any deep insight into what he really is, or what drives him on. We could not have been: it is not that there is something hidden in his soul. It is notable that he has no self-reflective aria – he never sings about himself, as Mozart's other central characters do. We have no sense of what he is like when he is by himself. He is presented always in action – the action, notoriously, of a seducer. The facts that the opera is of great and unsettling power, that a seducer is at the centre of it, and that the seducer is virtually characterless, were brought together in one of the first and most important reflections on the wider significance of the work, Søren Kierkegaard's famous essay 'The Immediate Stages of the Erotic, or The Musical Erotic'. It was one of a set of essays that he published in 1843. They were not published under his own name; Kierkegaard appears under a pseudonym, and even under this he claims only to introduce two sets of papers, by authors 'A' and 'B'. The papers of 'A' present an aesthetic view of life, those of 'B' an ethical view. The disjunction between the two views – the 'Either/Or' of the book's title – is left before the reader. Through all this indirection, the account of *Don Giovanni* is of course Kierkegaard's; but the authorial evasions are important, and they encourage him, or permit him, to leave a central question unresolved.

It is important that Kierkegaard is writing about Mozart's opera, and not merely about the character of Don Juan in general. This is not simply because he regards Mozart's as the greatest embodiment of the character. Beyond that, he thinks that it is a basic truth about the character that this should be so, a truth which he tries to explain. Mozart's is the greatest embodiment because of a perfect match of medium and content: music is the most 'abstract' of the arts, and is therefore ideally suited to express the abstract principle of sensual desire itself. And since that principle is what, above all, music expresses, *Don Giovanni* will also be the greatest work of music, a consequence which, amid a good deal of ironical self-reproof about the absurdity of such judgments, Kierkegaard (or rather his surrogate 'A') more or less allows himself.

Giovanni is the spirit of sensuous desire. He is (in a characteristic phrase) 'flesh incarnate'. He represents the third, full, and final stage of three forms of sensual interest, each of which has been represented by Mozart. The first, 'dreaming', is expressed in the tranquillity, the 'hushed melancholy', of Cherubino's feeling; the second, 'seeking', in Papageno's craving for discovery. Giovanni combines and goes beyond both of these attitudes, in full desire, in conquest. He is a seducer, yet it is not really he who seduces – rather 'he desires, and that desire acts seductively'. His is no particular or individual voice. It is the voice of all desire, and it speaks to all women: it is heard 'through the longing of all womanhood'. This is why Zerlina, the one woman whose attempted seduction is actually enacted for us, is rightly, and intentionally, an 'insignificant' character. Yet this conclusion itself raises a doubt. Zerlina has less to her than the other two women, and what in her responds to Giovanni – to his charm, his desire, and, as is made perfectly clear, his rank and money – is nothing very deeply hidden. Giovanni had been called upon on other occasions, surely, to exercise that more searching appeal of the stranger, which is brilliantly evoked in the novel by John Berger called *G*, one of the latest re-enactments of the Don Juan theme – and also one in which the figure appears at his most anonymously impersonal:

The stranger who desires you and convinces you it is truly you in all your particularity whom he desires, brings a message from all that you might be, to you as you actually are. Impatience to receive that message will be almost as strong as your sense of life itself. The desire to know oneself passes curiosity. But he must be a stranger, for the better you, that you actually are, know him, and likewise the better he knows you, the less he can reveal to you of your unknown but possible self. He must be a stranger.

In Zerlina it is no great distance to her unknown but possible self. It is a pity, one might feel, that Mozart did not enact for us the seduction of Donna Elvira – still more, of Donna Anna. According to E. T. A. Hoffmann's famous story, he did. Hoffmann represents Anna as actually seduced by Giovanni, and this fact as the ground of her response to him: 'She was not saved! when he rushed forth the deed was done. The fire of a superhuman sensuality, glowing from Hell, flowed through her innermost being and made her impotent to resist. Only he, only Don Juan, could arouse in her the lustful abandon with which she embraced him...'.

(see below, p. 130). The idea that Anna succumbed to Giovanni had been anticipated by Goldoni; but the significance that Hoffmann gives to this idea, and the consequences of it for the character and power of Giovanni, are what make Hoffmann's tale more than an anecdotal ·extension of the traditional plot.

Kierkegaard writes:

But what is this force then by which Don Juan seduces? It is the power of desire, the energy of sensual desire. He desires in every woman the whole of womanhood, and therein lies the sensually idealizing power with which he at once embellishes and overcomes his prey. The reflex of his gigantic passion beautifies and develops its object, who flushes in enhanced beauty by its reflection. As the fire of ecstasy with its seductive splendor illumines even the stranger who happens to have some relation to him, so he transfigures in a far deeper sense every girl, since his relation to her is an essential one. Therefore all finite differences fade away before him in comparison with the main thing: being a woman. He rejuvenates the older woman into the beautiful middle-age of womanhood: he matures the child almost instantly: everything which is woman is his prey. On the other hand, we must by no means understand this as if his sensuality were blind; instinctively he knows very well how to discriminate, and above all, he idealizes.

The idea that Giovanni is in pursuit of the ideal was to have a good deal of later history; a similar representation of his aims was given by Théophile Gautier, who wrote, 'It is not vulgar debauchery that drives him on; he seeks the dream of his heart with the obstinacy of a Titan who fears neither thunder nor lightning.' It is one way of trying to express the true conviction that Giovanni, in his musical embodiment, means more than Giovanni, in his character as tireless seducer, could actually manage to be. But it does that in the wrong way. It betrays the opera by still resting firmly in the terms of masculine pursuit. The feminine appears still as an object, even though it is idealized – perhaps all the more so because it is idealized. That result cannot be adequate to Mozart's work. *Don Giovanni* is a story about a seducer, indeed about *the* seducer, and has him as hero, but no sensible person could think that it was a work that represented women as more passive than men, or as deriving the point of their existence only from being the object, especially the idealized object, of some essentially masculine principle. This is above all because it gives such a powerful sense of the individuality and the desires of the women in it.

The Romantic airlessness of 'the ideal' suffocates both the individuality and the desires of women. It has been suggested, in fact, that there is just one respect in which the seducer – the real seducer, who pursues women and not the ideal — is one who himself affirms the liberty of women: though he exploits or even destroys them, he does decline to imprison them in a possessive institution. Although he 'has' them or 'makes' them, he does not make them his. The catalogue, as Jean Massin has said, is the negation of the harem.

If we are to give Giovanni his full stature, the erotic principle with which he is identified needs to be taken in some sense which is more general, and at the same time more honestly realistic, than the pursuit of the 'feminine ideal'. Kierkegaard himself seems to realize this, for later in his essay Giovanni is associated more generally with 'exuberant joy of life'. All the other characters have, compared with him, only a 'derived existence': he is 'the life principle within them'. It is the idea of Giovanni as a principle of vitality which explains, for instance, Leporello's attachment to him: he is absorbed, involved, swept up by him. Some idea of Giovanni as embodying the 'life force' is of course also what Shaw offers in *Man and Superman*; but in that enactment, seductive power and attractiveness have been replaced by a boundless loquacity, and the life force is extinguished among disquisitions on Darwinism and mournfully parochial paradoxes about the predatoriness of women. The Preface of the play is only too appropriately subscribed: 'Woking, 1903'.

Now that Giovanni has come to be identified with something as general as the living principle of all the characters, the centre of their vitality, a difficulty arises; and since that identification has something right about it, and expresses convincingly Giovanni's musical relation to the rest of the opera, it is a real difficulty, which everyone has to face. Has Giovanni any longer a relation to either the social order or an order of divine judgment? When he was just a finite and particular kind of sexual brigand, there was no mystery in the idea that he should be hunted, prosecuted, or damned; but when he has taken on this larger and more abstract significance, is there anything left to the idea of an order against which he is to be judged? In particular, what do we make of his end?

There is no clear or adequate answer to this question in Kierkegaard's own essay. He indeed notably plays down Giovanni's nastiness — he denies that he is really a schemer or even a deceiver, just because he is always energy in action, unselfconsciousness. When Giovanni becomes as idealized as this — so that he seems an innocent, the *Erdgeist,* a male, active, and unvictimized Lulu — the question of the order that condemns him becomes a very pressing one. Kierkegaard tell us, in effect, only that Giovanni is opposed to the spirit of Christianity, which is also (by a highly Hegelian identification) reflective spirit. This leaves us with an excessively blank fact, that Giovanni is breaking Christian laws and that is why he is punished. But that hardly says enough, even to Christians, if Giovanni indeed represents everyone's living principle. Kierkegaard himself perhaps escapes this criticism because he offers us in the essay only the view of 'A', the aesthetic view of life, and it is hardly surprising that he gestures only remotely towards the ethical. But the ethical will have to be got into closer relation to Giovanni than this, if Giovanni is everything that 'A' says that he is.

In distinguishing Mozart's Giovanni from an intriguer, Kierkegaard explicitly distinguishes him from Molière's Don Juan. That figure is driven particularly by the fear of boredom, the attempt to overcome satiation. Molière is mainly responsible for the idea of Don Juan as the amatory strategist, the hunter who is above all concerned with the tactics of the chase. It was a theme taken up later by Stendhal, who himself, however, finally pronounced in favour of Werther as opposed to Don Juan, the sentimental rather than the strategic. Stendhal's contrast, of course, relates simply to love – as something made, at any rate, if not felt. But the ruthless pursuer of love can come to represent, rather than one type of lover, one type of pursuer.

Simone de Beauvoir has said: 'If existentialism were solipsistic, the adventurer would be its perfect hero', and Giovanni is one type of the adventurer. He is a kind of nihilist, on this reading: one who indeed denies God and the fetishism of conventional moral approval and social rewards, and who lives through free action for its own sake. He represents 'the union of an original abundant vitality and reflective scepticism', but unlike the genuine and committed existentialist hero he has no sense of freedom as something all should share, and hence, like an adventurer in another style, Pizarro, he has contempt for other people. At the same time, he is dependent, dialectically, on social institutions which he rejects – wealth, and the liberty given by class.

Da Ponte constantly reminds us that Giovanni is a member of the nobility and that he deploys his rank and, as he himself very explicitly reminds us, his money, to get what he wants. He belongs of course to the equally noble world of Don Ottavio and Donna Anna, but we are left in no doubt what his contempt is for such a world, as a social order. When Masetto sees Zerlina being taken away from him by Giovanni and is prevented by Leporello from following, his outburst (No. 6) combines the pains both of love and of social insult.

Formally there is a parallel here with the relations of Figaro and the Count, but there is also a basic difference. It is not only that Figaro is a complete person whereas Masetto is a more schematic and simpler character. Still less is it that Giovanni is the hero of his opera, while the Count is the villain of his – that oversimplifies our relations to both of them. Giovanni is not a hero we enter into, whereas, very strikingly, the point at which we are given the deepest and most sympathetic insight into the Count is in that aria ('Vedrò, mentr'io sospiro') in which he expresses the rage of baffled class power. The difference between the operas is that the Count and Figaro totally belong to the social world in which they are presented, and their motivations are naturally related to that world, whereas Giovanni is only making use of the social world in which he was born, and is basically a solitary figure who exploits but does not belong to his social surroundings. He is a brigand within his own country. He is at ease in being so, and Mozart is at ease in re- presenting him so. While Giovanni is using his position, there is surely no ambivalence in it, or in the opera's attitude to it, such as Ernst Bloch suggested, who found in it the mark of 'a strangely ambiguous titanism' (*eines merkwürdig gesprenkelten Titanismus*), and asked, 'Is Don Giovanni, as Mozart shows him, a wolf or a human face under so many masks? Does he belong fully to the society of the Ancien Régime, as its most ruthless representative, or do we detect in him, in the erotic ex- plosive rebellion, part of a return to nature?' Giovanni certainly lives off the land, but does so in an individual way that firmly refuses any such historical question. That he exploits others is identified by Simone de Beauvoir as a contradiction in the adventurer's situation – he both denies and affirms the need of his social background. But this is so, surely, only if he intends, or someone intends, his style of life to be an expression of freedom as something which everyone might try to follow. Giovanni himself entertains no such aspiration, nor does he reject it: he is not reflective in that style at all.

Nor in any other. It is this that marks him off from another great embodiment of reckless human energy with whom he has indeed been associated, Faust. A German author, Christian Dietrich Grabbe, produced in 1829 a play (*Don Juan und Faust*) which brought the two heroes to- gether, a meeting which involves the following rather plodding exchange:

Don Juan:	Wozu übermenschlich Wenn du ein Mensch bleibst?
Faust:	Wozu Mensch Wenn du nach übermenschlichem nicht strebst?
Don Juan:	What is the point of the superhuman If you remain man?
Faust:	What is the point of man If you do not strive for the superhuman?

Such solemnities do not belong to the world of Giovanni. Even without them, Faust's undertaking, because it is essentially reflective, differs from Giovanni's. It is not merely that he is a scholar and an experimentalist, though that is true, and his attitude to Helen or Gretchen is of that kind – he loves or seduces as an experiment or an experience, in order to have done so, and that is the opposite of Giovanni, who simply says that he needs women 'more than I need the food that I eat or the air that I breathe' (II.1). More basically, Faust's whole bargain – what makes him the over-reacher he is – is reflective: it is a product of the calculation of the values of finite and infinite, and that is not a kind of enterprise known to Giovanni. As Camus remarked, Giovanni does not really believe in the after-life, unlike Faust 'who believed enough in God to sell himself to the devil'.

But this leads us back to the questions about Giovanni's end; and whether it is, despite the opera's first title, *Il dissoluto punito,* a punishment. If the Commendatore is the veritable voice of Heaven, a Christian Sarastro, so to speak, then Giovanni's defiance of him, the refusal of repentance in the face of a manifest miracle, is awesomely perverse. The celebration of Giovanni as Promethean hero, or – as by Musset and by Baudelaire, for example – as a figure of fascinating satanic evil, will then be in place.[2] But Giovanni is not a satanic evil figure, and the extraordinary power his musical image expresses is not that of a tragic hero either. Camus is again to the point:

Don Juan would find it natural that he should be punished. It is the rule of the game. And it is exactly a mark of his generosity, to have entirely accepted the rule of the game. But he knows that he is right, and that there can be no question of punishment. An inevitable end is not the same thing as a penalty.

If Giovanni's wilful defiance does not have a luciferian significance, then what he is defying cannot be God. The Commendatore in stone is on any showing an impressive figure: Shaw said that those trombones were 'a sound of dreadful joy to all musicians'. But his is not the voice of God. He is made of stone, and he does not come from Heaven (whatever he says about his diet), but from the churchyard where we first heard him. He is a terrible and unforeseen natural consequence of Giovanni's recklessness. He is indeed *super*natural, but only in the sense of a realm of cause and effects which lie beyond the natural, not one that brings a new order of guilt and judgment. Giovanni's lofty refusal to repent when the statue demands that he should is not an ultimate offence to the cosmic order, but rather a splendidly attractive and grand refusal to be intimidated.

If Giovanni's refusal were to be Faustian *hubris* or Promethean defiance, as some Romantic writers wanted, it would have to be something that he had come to after consideration. Mozart's tempi reveal it as convinced, but not as considered. The Commendatore's andante gives Giovanni time to repent, but he does not give himself time, and could not do so. He is always in action; even when he is resting from one adventure, he is in flight for the next. His natural speed, throughout the opera, is that of 'Eh via buffone' (No. 14) (rather slower than 'Fin ch'an dal vino' (No. 11), a piece designed to show that even he can accelerate). That speed is not right for reflection; and no composer has ever found it the right speed for Faust. Shaw's Don Juan, by contrast, becalmed in that limitless lagoon of talk, loses his entire *raison d'être*.

The Commendatore does not need to be the voice of God; and the devils' chorus scarcely *could* be the sound of the Christian Inferno. The final sextet even refers to the place to which Don Giovanni has been removed, not by any Christian phrase, but in terms of the old creaking classical machinery of Proserpina and Pluto: da Ponte attached no very great weight to that, no doubt, but it is quite right. Those old gods were themselves part of nature, and Giovanni's great virtue of courage, which he expressly boasts in his last moments, is displayed in a marvellous piece of consistency, of sufficiency, of bravado – a very proper and fine human reaction to something which, granted indeed his wicked life, is of the order of a vast and alarming natural consequence, rather than a transcendental judgment.

Curiously, each of Mozart's great Italian comedies has something unsatisfactory or problematic about its end. None of them perfectly solves the problem raised by its own depth – the problem of relating to the defining normality of comedy the intensity that the work has given to the irregular. Each promises a return to normality which it fails to define properly; each embodies some emotion which does not quite match the past or the future. In *Figaro*, there is the problem that at the end of the 'mad day', the Count and the Countess express reconciliation and forgiveness in music of such rapturous beauty that it can only be saying that all will be well for ever, when we know, from everything we have seen, that it cannot be for more than a week. In *Così fan tutte*, everybody is rattled back to their right partners in a manner which, granted what we have just been shown, can only be totally heartless. In *Don Giovanni* the final sextet represents, very explicitly, a return to ordinary life. Should we take that to mean: a return to the ordinary as against the supernatural, which has just done its work? Or a return to the decent with the end of the wicked?

There is certainly a return to the expected, after the intervention of the extraordinary. But that return does not define what has disappeared as simply wicked, indecent, or unnecessary. In fact, the characters, with the exception of Zerlina and Masetto, scarcely do 'return to normal', but rather try to stick something together from what is left now that Giovanni has gone. Life without him will not merely be life with the wicked satisfactorily punished. Although his punishment is the subject of the closing words of the finale, and the moral of its 'antichissima canzon', Mozart has already shown us that life without Giovanni will be life that has lost a very powerful and single-minded embodiment of qualities which are indeed human. Because he was *just* those qualities, he himself lacked humanity – he was without love, compassion, and fairness, to mention only a few of the things that he lacked. But the relation of what he had to what he lacked cannot be adequately expressed simply in terms of vice and virtue, dissoluteness and punishment, and that is something that Kierkegaard's interpretation half sees – sees, one might say, with half of him; but his essay leaves us, inadequately, still with the punishment as a blank requirement of the Christian consciousness, besides contributing the ultimately sterile idea, favoured by some Romantics, that Giovanni's pursuit of women was more than it seemed because it was the pursuit of the ideal woman.

Contrary to that, other Romantics found his heroism in a displacement of ordinary virtue: face to face with the cosmic order, he defiantly, tragically, or even satanically, rejects it. That account of him both overestimates the transcendental character of what he confronts, and underestimates the simply human, recognizable, and invigorating quality of his attitude to that confrontation.

The sense of freedom that he expresses does not have all the metaphysical resonances that existentialist writers found in it, but it does have a significance which goes beyond an individual personal characteristic, and so does his recklessness. His single-minded determination to live at the fullest energy, at the extreme edge of desire, neglects consequences to himself as much as to others. Granted what makes life valuable to him, the ultimate consequences are irrelevant: cowardice, for him, would simply involve a misunderstanding of what was worth pursuing, just as considerateness (unless things happened to take him that way) would be a distraction. He understands perfectly well that society exists – he can skilfully negotiate its obstacles. He understands that other people exist – how else could he so unfailingly find the 'unknown but possible self' of all those women? He has a perfectly clear idea of what might destroy him – his end was not just a mistake.

That end, however, and still more the essential closing bars of the opera
that follow it, both affirm that there is no actual human life that could
be lived as unconditionally as his. Those who survive Giovanni – not
only the other characters, but, on each occasion that we have seen the
opera, ourselves – are both more and less than he is: more, since the
conditions *on* humanity, which we accept, are also the conditions *of*
humanity; and less, since one thing vitality needs is to keep the dream
of being as free from conditions as his.

7 The music

An ensemble of perplexity; the quartet

The quartet No. 9 is a turning-point in *Don Giovanni*, articulated by a marvel of restrained expression and musically controlled confusion. Even in Mozart's ensembles or finales continuity of action is seldom precisely synchronized with the demands of musical form. The admirable analyses by Kerman and Rosen of the trio (No. 15), and the sextet show how Mozart's ensembles derive dramatic and musical strength from their re-lationship to the classical design known as sonata form.[1] In the trio, for example, the action for two-thirds of the piece proceeds at something like a realistic pace: exposition, Elvira on the balcony, the men below; development, Giovanni's persuasion, her anger and yielding, Leporello's suppressed mirth. But the recapitulation suspends time for the charac-ters to explore their inner feelings. This constantly shifting relationship of action and musical necessity is subtler than what Kerman calls the 'frank convention' of baroque opera, in which action is recitative, con-templation aria; but it is not the less a convention. In the quartet the sonata design is adapted to the dramatic development which takes place as it unfolds. In Scene 11 Giovanni begins to play confidently on the feelings of Anna and Ottavio, hoping to direct their suspicions else-where. Elvira returns with her 'At it again' (sc. 12) and begins the quar-tet when she turns to warn Anna. Later she and Giovanni compete to persuade the others, who stand aside, only half involved. Remarks are exchanged aloud or in whispers; some lines are asides. This suggests con-siderable comic stage movement, but there are some static patches where two or four characters are soliloquizing.

The text consists of twelve quatrains (longer than the sextet; an aria normally has only two). They fall into four groups which correspond with the musical sections: exposition, A tonic section, B move to, and cadence in, the dominant; development modulating; recapitulation, tonic. The first group presents the opening gambits. Elvira speaks to Anna (1: 'Non ti fidar. . .'); the couple react (2: 'Cieli! che aspetto nobile! '); Giovanni, aside to the couple (but Elvira listens), begins to spin the tale (3: 'La povera ragazza . . .') (see above, Chapter 2, for the synopsis, and below, Exx. 1 and 2). Giovanni's verse has minor differences in structure, and begins in a different musical tone, but, characteristically for Mozart, the group is all in the tonic with a cadence at the end of each quatrain. The second group of three quatrains begins with a rapid exchange of single lines (4: 'Ah, non credete al perfido': Elvira: 'Don't believe him'; Giovanni: 'She is mad, don't listen'; Elvira: 'Do not go away'; the couple: 'Whom to believe? '). Quatrains 5 and 6 have identical second and fourth lines. Giovanni is in unison with the couple, in rhythm as well as words (5: 'Certo moto d'ignoto tormento' (Giovanni: 'spavento')). Elvira has more verbal variation and her music is quite distinct (6: 'Sdegno, rabbia. . .'). This is soliloquy; while in quatrain 4 the tonal action matches the acceleration of exchanges by moving to the dominant, F, in 5 and 6 it remains in that key, ending the exposition with a firm cadence (bar 49).

The third group begins with two-line asides, except that Elvira characteristically breaks the pattern by uttering aloud. In quatrain 7 Ottavio declares that he will not budge until the matter is cleared up; Anna says that Elvira's features and speech do not suggest madness (see below, Ex. 3). In quatrain 8, to the same musical pattern, Giovanni remarks that if he leaves, the others will suspect ('Se men vado . . .'); Elvira ('Da qual ceffo . . .') denounces him: 'You can see from his face how black is his soul.' The group ends with quatrain 9, mostly half-line asides:

Ottavio:	Dunque quella?	
Giovanni:		E pazzarella.
Anna:	Dunque quegli?	
Elvira:		E un traditore.
Giovanni:	Infelice!	
Elvira:		Mentitore!
Anna, Ottavio:	Incomincio a dubitar.	
Ottavio:	So she is . . .?	
Giovanni:		A lunatic.
Anna:	So he is . . .?	
Elvira:		A betrayer.
Giovanni:	Poor thing!	
Elvira:		Liar!
Anna, Ottavio:	I begin to have my doubts.	

The last line for the *opera seria* couple, embroiled in this *buffo* quartet with deadly undertones, is obviously crucial. As usual in a development the music is intensified by rapid key-changes; by quatrain 8 it has reached the dominant, in preparation for the return to B flat.

The final group begins with Giovanni, much perturbed, hissing at

Elvira to keep quiet (10: 'Zitto, zitto'). She replies *forte* that she has
abandoned prudence (11: 'Non sperarlo, o scellerato'). These quatrains
are reiterated while the couple add their own aside, Anna watching Giovanni (12: 'Quegli accenti si sommessi': 'These whispers, this change of
colour, show clearly which is in the right'). Sonata form demands a recapitulation here of the first key and theme. In opera, unless the situation suggests otherwise, this may be only the recovery of the key. Thus
in the trio, Elvira returns to her original softened mood, and her original
melody; but in the sextet there is no melodic reprise, only an emphatic
tonic section presented in a new tempo (see above, p. 48). In the quartet
there is no melodic reprise, unless it is of Elvira's aria (No. 3); the violin
figures in bars 70-2 are similar gestures of wrath and impatience. Only
at the end does Anna return to the principal motif of the first section,
and this delay of the reprise has some dramatic significance.

The details of this broad design are full of subtlety. Elvira begins by
breaking free of the abusive language both of No. 8 and of her entrance
line; she gathers herself by hovering on the D which is the initiating
note of the principal motifs of the quartet. As a result a five-bar ante-

Ex. 1

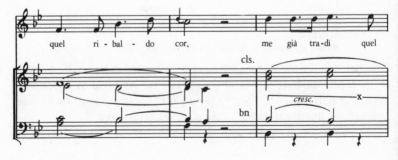

cedent phrase is given a four-bar consequent of far more decisive musical character; Elvira has sized Anna up, and events prove the rightness of her chosen approach (Ex. 1). Mozart's concern for organic musical growth, and his dramatic need to show the others' reaction to Elvira's incursion, gentle in manner but startling in content, lead to the echo of 'y' (see Ex. 1, bars 9ff): 'Te vuol tradir ancor', a warning just as No. 8 was to Zerlina. Its graceful shape hovers over the rest of the piece. It accompanies a musically nebulous four-bar antecedent in quatrain 2 (lines 1–2), and as Anna takes it up in the consequent (line 4) we know that Elvira is winning already. As a result, and in contrast to the way the characters are introduced in the sextet, Anna and Ottavio almost reduplicate Elvira's music, condensing her nine bars into eight, then repeating the cadence to make ten. They are bound to Elvira by the four consecutive statements of 'y' (bars 8–11), and a triple statement (bars 16–18) ends the section, which thus acts as a decisive confirmation of Elvira's music. Giovanni sings to a dry chromatic unison, but his music drifts inexorably to a further confirmation of Elvira's. The chromatic line comes from bars 6–7 ('x' in Ex. 1), a counterpoint actually sung at that pitch by Giovanni in bars 23–4; and bar 25, rising to the germinal pitch of the opening, is so close to 'y' that a twofold statement of 'y' follows naturally as if to mock him (Ex. 2). Try as Giovanni may to formulate

Ex. 2

his own musical idea, he can only complement Elvira's, so that the form so far is in effect strophic. He is rattled; the tale of madness comes too easily and carries even less conviction than before since the music achieves no more than a counterpoint to the moral force of Elvira.[2]

Elvira's self-possession is hard-won, and she too loses it (although not too obviously, as Anna's remark in quatrain 7 tells us). She retains her assertiveness, however, and her impulsive 'Ah, non credete al perfido' begins the move to the dominant which Giovanni completes, still flowing with her tide. As Anna and Ottavio reiterate the close on F and move to its dominant Elvira (bar 33) builds an arpeggio inverting Giovanni's (bar 32) which trumpets forth on the C major chord (bar 35). During the ensemble (quatrains 5-6) she breaks into flourishes of abuse between the joint soliloquy of the others in which Giovanni is subservient, providing only a bass or a counterpoint of little character while the couple engage in an impressive imitation of the chromatic motif (bars 40-3). Mozart takes care that this section introduces no new motif of striking character, for he has no space for the necessary recapitulation of such an idea in the main key; but he makes it a central climax through this chromatic imitation and Elvira's *fioriture*.

As so often when sonata-type structures are applied to dramatic music, the most evidently dramatic section, the 'development', is the shortest. The quatrains are rushed through without word repetition, and with no more than a momentary overlapping of phrases. Mozart smoothes the rapid modulatory exchange by fourfold use of a new idea, but he

Ex. 3

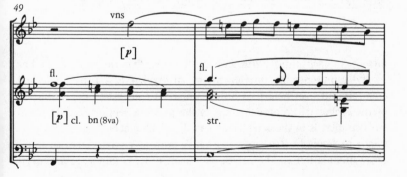

introduces each phrase with an accented minim on the half-bar (cf. bar 1) and represents the puzzlement of all (except Elvira) by a winding counterpoint over held bass notes, a marked contrast to the simplicity of the orchestral accompaniment in the previous section (Ex. 3). Ottavio's couplet is in the established key, F, which makes Anna's turn to C minor particularly affecting. Giovanni's growing anxiety leads to an intense modulation to the minor dominant of C, G minor; Elvira, deci-

sively, goes to the tonic, B flat. The point of having each phrase virtually the same is that each is a private utterance; the exception, Elvira,
who is not puzzled and who makes her remark to Anna, is all the more
marked. Her closure in B flat brings something like 'y' (second violins
and flute: the tritone E flat − A closing in on B flat, but the initial D is
missing).[3] The next set of exchanges is all on the dominant; a good deal
of position-changing on stage is probably necessary. Giovanni turns the
music towards B flat minor, and is mocked in this, one of his few direct-
ing gestures in the piece, when Elvira's violent onslaught on the dominant, and on him, reiterates this inflection: 'Mentitore', giving him the
lie direct. Finally Anna and Ottavio float down in parallel thirds in an
augmentation of the scale-figure which began the section, landing on
the dominant as if ready to resolve their doubts (the last section certainly implies that they believe Elvira).

Giovanni, although seriously disturbed, contrives to divert his enemy
at the last moment. In a sinuous unison, which brings the music back to
the tonic B flat, he initiates the last section, whispering in the exaggerated
parlando style of Leporello that she should not create a scandal (quatrain 10).[4] His recovery enables him to end the piece slanging it out
with Elvira, and no doubt, as Mozart's diminuendo suggests, manoeuvr-
ing her away from the others. But his victory is his undoing; his anger
and alarm are too obvious, and it needs only a press of the hand, a too
gallant leave-taking, for Anna's suspicions to become certainty. Elvira
may seem to give in when she is winning, but her victory is as complete
as when she removed Zerlina; this too is clear in the music. Giovanni
may lead back to the tonic (bar 70) but it is Elvira who characterizes its
recovery with her sharp phrases, which only superficially resemble his
buffo style, for their effect is harsh, abrasive; moreover they prolong
the section by their aggressive thrust towards the dominant. When Anna
and Ottavio join in they work steadily through a crescendo to bar 78 and
debouch into a reprise of the original consequent in its entirety (bars 79-
82; cf. bars 6-9 in Ex. 1). In what were previously pregnant silences
Elvira is heard, still *forte*: 'Ho perduto la prudenza' (bar 80). Thereafter
she is quieter and Giovanni, who from bar 74 was tied to a dominant
pedal and rhythms complementing those of the couple, now fills the
gaps between cadences. But his apparent ascendancy is denied by the
ubiquity of 'y', which is passed between Anna and the orchestra (bars
81-5) and is then given twice more in the coda, going from violins to an
octave coupling of clarinet and flute, the instruments which successively
took the phrase in bars 10-11. What was inherent there is realized here;
Elvira's warning has sunk deeply in.

Mozartian characterization

Some say that the quartet is the last debt to Bertati before the graveyard scene; but it is exactly in this ensemble that da Ponte showed his
superior imagination and seriousness, as well as wit. Mozart supported
him fully. The dominant personality is Elvira, so the quartet is coloured
by the instrumentation of No. 3 (plus a flute). After the Overture the
clarinets are silent until No. 3, then again until the quartet. Both movements omit oboes, which play everywhere else (except in No. 8, scored
for strings only). This orchestral characterization is pursued when
Mozart omits the clarinets from No. 10; full woodwind is used in No.
11 for the first time since the Overture. In Act II the sextet also uses
full wind, but the clarinets rest at the entrance of Anna and Ottavio
(Elvira is silent). The clarinets are not confined to flat keys; No. 15 is in
A, an Elvira piece with clarinets and no oboes. The association of clarinets with Elvira is weakened by 'Il mio tesoro' and 'Non mi dir', with
their delectable clarinet parts (neither has oboes). Nevertheless the connection with Elvira is strong, for Mozart reverted to it in composing No.
21b. This careful distinction between the two 'equally good Frauenzim-
merrollen' (see above, p. 6) is pursued in their manner of singing, and is
clear when they sing together in the apparently homogeneous trio of
maskers (No. 13.5) (Ex. 4). Anna's virtuosity consists of elegantly

Ex. 4

cor!   Pro - teg - ga il giu - sto   cie - lo

- mor!   Ven - dichi, ven-dichi il giu - sto   cie - lo,

Anna: May the justice of heaven protect my heart's zeal!
Elvira: May the justice of heaven avenge my slighted love!

sweeping scales, Elvira's of widely spanning, angular arpeggiation, recall-
ing the coda to No. 3 and the end of the quartet's exposition (bars 45-
8). Even at the end of 'Non mi dir' Anna's music has a poise missing in
the flashing scales which end that astonishing invention, No. 8.

Nos. 8 and 9 show the opposite poles of Elvira. In No. 8 she admon-
ishes a peasant girl; Dent was reminded of a sermon.[5] The style has
rightly been identified as archaic, and Mozart cannot have been un-
aware that he was, not for the first time, composing 'in Handelian style'.
When she perceives that Anna is her social equal, Elvira adopts a tone of
persuasion, almost palpably getting a grip on herself at 'Non ti fidar. . .'
(see above, Ex. 1). This owes nothing to Bertati, or Molière; nor are the
words so very different from those she used to Zerlina. One could hardly find a better demonstration of the truism that in opera the composer
is the dramatist.

The fascination and vividness of Elvira lie in this volatile *mezzo carattere*. Her vehemence and tenderness emerge from the depths of love
and shame, and alternate in any number long enough to accommodate
both (Nos. 3, 9, 15, 24.3). Both sensuous and pious, she is thoroughly
mixed in her motives; her interventions derive their effectiveness from
jealousy as well as altruism. Her adaptability makes her like Giovanni,
his complementary opposite (as Leporello is his shadow): constant in
love where he is changeable, changeable in intention where he is constant. The strength of her love is her undoing and her triumph, for
while it lets her be fooled it also permits the moral victory of final re-
nunciation. There is no practical result; her feelings overwhelm her, she
is incoherent, and Giovanni is amused rather than moved (No. 24.3).
But this Elvira is more human than any of her prototypes.

The interpolated aria No. 21b is often, and understandably, considered an excrescence. It may be justified as forming a bridge between
Elvira's humiliation in No. 19 and her intervention in the finale. Ker-

man remarks that she 'becomes the most interesting of the ladies on account of the progress in her lyrical utterances – but only with the help of a thoroughly gratuitous aria, "Mi tradì. . ." '. In fact similar progress, although it has even less effect on the action, is to be seen in Anna through 'Non mi dir', a scene which Dent said 'has no reason whatever for its existence'. Brophy says of 'Mi tradì' that 'it has a sublimated cheerfulness in torment worthy of Saint Lawrence, and a merry-go-round quality of simply keeping going, which precisely illustrates the intense and unendurable circling of Donna Elvira's feelings'. Would this suffice to justify Cavalieri's insistence on another aria, and, since it indubitably accomplishes what Kerman calls a 'clear psychological progression', render it not gratuitous after all?[6]

As is to be expected of a *seria* role, Anna is less complex and there is no real evidence of mixed motives. It is the force of her determination which leads to dispute as to its cause and the nature of her relations with Ottavio and Giovanni (the latter hardly affected by the unanswerable question of whether she was actually seduced). In fact, only her first words in the *scena ultima* (see above, p. 64) are inconsistent with the portrait of a tender, deeply affronted, but loving young woman. The music supports this at every turn; in the accompanied recitatives which (with Elvira's in No. 21b) are among the glories of *Don Giovanni*, and above all in the arias. The noble 'Or sai chi l'onore' (No. 10), with its sombre reiterated cry for vengeance, includes a deeply affecting recollection of her father's death (see below, p. 117). 'Non mi dir' comes when, with vengeance impending, she can consider the future; her wish to honour her father in the eyes of the world, which has aroused criticism, springs from recognition that he can only be properly honoured by such public sacrifice; we should not read indifference into this merely because modern customs are so different. She loves Ottavio; the recitative and aria cannot be understood otherwise. Music cannot lie. If Mozart and da Ponte wanted us to understand, here and in Act I Scene 13 when she narrates her experiences to Ottavio, that Anna is a liar and a hypocrite, they could have found some way for music and text to contradict each other. They did not. The end of the recitative of No. 23 is full of the pain which refusal causes her (Ex. 5). The flat supertonic (Neapolitan: 'N') has seldom been more heartrending, as Anna floats to her highest note; then falling to C sharp, poignant with the appoggiatura ('A'), she does not go to the obvious next note, D, but by a diminished interval to F, further intensified by the diminished seventh chord ('X'). The musical language has nothing novel; but it concentrates expressive devices which Mozart, more than most, dared to withhold until they

Ex. 5

Anna

oh Di - o!   Non   se - dur la mia co - stan - za del sen-

- si - bil mio co-re!   Ab - ba-stan - za per   te   mi   par - la a - mo - re.

in G minor: VI
in D minor: N

meant most, and then used together for their mutual enhancement. As
for 'Non mi dir' itself, it is not usually pointed out that Berlioz's notorious hatred for its final coloratura derived from his keen appreciation
of the beauty of the larghetto, 'of a profound sadness, where all the
poetry of love stands forth in tears and mourning'.[7] The scene is thus
no mere interlude between the two statue scenes, but an integral part of
the relationship of the *opera seria* characters, one of an interest and intensity most unusual in that genre.

Finally, the title-role. From the musical point of view the problem is
that this allegedly Faustian (or better, Mephistophelian) 'hero' speaks

almost exclusively in the idiom of *opera buffa*. It is part of his technique to adapt himself to his interlocutor, but this *buffo* idiom extends beyond the scenes with Leporello, who, decidedly, sets the tone of their duets (Nos. 14 and 22). Giovanni has no long aria; Leporello's (No.4) is of course entirely concerned with the master's exploits, but it is a servant's piece. In secco recitative the two bandy words on equal terms, in *buffo* style, and are distinguished not in idiom but in vocal type, the light gentlemanly baritone and the plebeian bass. Although many fine basses have sung Giovanni, they really have no business to; it weakens the comedy of these two imitating each other (Act II, Scenes 3-5 and 7) and does not fit the musical conception.

Leporello is a real person, as are the peasants, ladies, and even Ottavio. Because of the music, Giovanni's reality is more doubtful. His 'credo' is delivered mockingly, in secco recitative (Act II Scene 1; see above, pp. 17 and 88); there is no need to take this sophistry seriously, although some have done so.[8] Certainly it suggests no very spiritual attitude to the game of conquest. The only modification of Giovanni's high-spirited heartlessness, and *buffo* style, comes in the extreme scenes, Nos. 1 and 24; and it is really no exception, for he is still taking another's musical cue, but here it is the Commendatore's. In No. 1, confronted with uprightness and courage, the blackguard adopts the same tone, agreeing to fight with a disdainful show of reluctance. The music changes abruptly at the Commendatore's entrance, and its character is impregnated with his grandly old-fashioned cadences (Ex. 6A). The

Ex. 6A

first, Phrygian, cadence ('P') is prominently used only once more in the opera, by Elvira (I.4; significantly just before Leporello says she talks like a book). The Commendatore brings about the modulations, to G minor at his entrance, then D minor (Ex. 6A), the key of the fight, and it is he who confirms F minor as he falls wounded (Ex. 6B). At this point Giovanni suddenly seems vulnerable, even real (it is in the music; there is no need to point crudely to the issue of the drama by a handclasp with the dying man). He sings a melody which was first given to Anna (Ex. 6C). This vulnerability appears only briefly in the first finale, where there is no intimation of mortality (see above, pp. 62ff); it is shrugged off by a friendly little violin tune at 'Ma non manca in me coraggio' (No. 13, bar 615). In the second finale Giovanni responds to his unbelievable visitor with dignity, although a moment before he was arguing on equal terms with Leporello. Finally, in response as much to the servant's 'Tell him no!' as to the statue's 'Verrai?' ('Shall I see

Ex. 6B

you?'), he accepts his destiny with real grandeur (Ex. 7). Even so the baroque dotted rhythm springing forth from the violins (hitherto the property of Elvira the moralist, No. 8) has the Commendatore's pomp.

Ex. 6C

Ex. 7

If this opera is partly about disguise, Giovanni is its master; but he is like an actor who has lost himself in his roles. In Act I his verbal masks are designed for Leporello, the peasants, and Anna; in Act II he plays the penitent for Elvira, the troubadour for her maid, and the servant for Masetto, in three consecutive numbers (15-17). In the last ('Metà di voi') he seems to forget the mask in the enjoyment of the action, allowing an aristocratic command to show through; whereas the opening of the aria is *parlando*, the suavity and delicate chromaticism of bars 57ff are outside Leporello's style.

Where is the real Giovanni? After 'Là ci darem' he admits to Elvira, with rare honesty, that 'io voglio divirtirmi' ('I just want a bit of fun'). The natural hedonist appears in the first finale, contributing everything material, but nothing human, to the festivity. In 'Fin ch'an dal vino', his nearest approach to a personal aria, he wears the mask of gallant hospitality, coupling unrestrained exuberance with delightfully aristocratic innuendo (compare bars 57ff with Leporello's outrageousness at the end of No. 4). No more than that other set of misleading directions, 'Metà di voi', does this develop him as a personality.

Giovanni needs Leporello as a shadow because he casts none of his own, so swiftly does he run. Almost he is spirit, not a man. Deliberately, Mozart allows him no depth (see above, p. 82). For Kerman this is a defect of the whole opera: 'To say that Don Giovanni's lack of involvement is precisely the strongest element of his personality is to argue *ab vacuo*; in opera we trust what is done most firmly by the music. The very blankness of Don Giovanni's characterization, indeed, must have been what especially attracted Romantic critics. Their daydreams and idealizations could sprout in Mozart's relative void.'[9] Not only Romantic critics, for the misunderstanding of Giovanni began earlier, with late-eighteenth-century German productions, and arose from a false sense of the need to develop the characterization. But Kerman does not say how lack of involvement could have been *firmly* done by the music. Self-evidently it could not. The grand aria sought by Bassi would have marred all, rendering the character more solid, but less demonic, more conventional, like Gazzaniga's. Among Mozart's feats of characterization must be included this, of having a man so much on stage, the centre of so many situations, with so much to sing, and yet making clear his vacuity. Although quite different, his Giovanni is the perfect counterpart to the empty, frigid atheist of Molière.

Large-scale musical structure

Tonality and tonal change are potent weapons in Mozart's arsenal of devices for intensifying the drama, and for filling the whole canvas of an opera with perspectives, cross-relationships, variety, and unity. Most obviously tonality will bind together a composite finale, a form which is one of the most individual achievements of *opera buffa*, and of which Mozart is unquestionably the supreme exponent. Space prohibits a full analysis of either finale, but an outline of the first (No. 13) will illustrate the point. It begins and ends in C major, and returns there once in the middle (Table 3). The most readily understood cross-references are melodic, but here they contribute little to the unity of the finale (the anticipation of two of the dances in 13.3 and 13.4; the use of a single figure in 13.9 (bar 479) and 13.11 (bar 549)). Tonal unity consists of variety grouped around one centre, 13.3. This is not melodically identified when it returns, and it is approached from different directions. One might wonder, therefore, how it can be *heard* as a return. Mozart provides what Tovey has called the necessary 'collateral evidence' in his instrumentation.[10] Giovanni's entrance (sc. 17, in 13.1) and the entrance of the maskers (13.7) are announced by trumpets and drums, whose

Table 3. *Finale I (No. 13)*

Section	1 Allegro		2 Andante	3 Allegretto (Contre-danse)		4 Minuet
Scene	16	17	18		19	
Action	Masetto, Zerlina	Giovan-ni Tpt, drum	Seduction; surprise	Trio; exeunt	Maskers	Leporello's invitation
Key	C	⟶	F		[d]	F ⟶

5 Adagio	Scene-change	6 Allegro	7 Maestoso	8 Minuet	9 Allegro	10 Andante	11 Allegro
		20					
Prayer		Quartet; revelry	Maskers Tpt, drum	Dance-scene	Outrage	Confron-tation	Freeze Tpt, drum
B♭ ⟶		E♭	C V → G		[E♭, b♭, c, V/d]	F V → C	

Capital letters: major keys
Small letters: minor keys
Letters in square brackets: keys used in passing
V: dominant

mechanical limitations prevent them playing in all the keys (this can be deceptive evidence: see the sextet, in which they enter in D, but later change to E flat). The connection is also made by the vigorous, martial character of the rhythms which the use of these instruments suggests. Even at the climax of excitement (13.9) they are not used; they return only with the tonic (13.11). Thus they provide enough vivid and *heard* similarity to assist the understanding of three diverse movements as three tonal pillars.

The immediate tonal steps differ significantly, and underline the central dramatic significance of this finale, which is not the attempt on Zerlina but the uniting of Giovanni's enemies. If we discount D minor (13.3) because it is enclosed within two passages of F major (related by the use of dance-music coming from the house into the garden), each step is down a fifth, the easiest and least intense of modulations between major keys because the first key becomes the dominant of the second (arrows in Table 3). This progression into flat keys covers the scene-change, whose possible disruptiveness is thus minimized (its dramatic significance is slight). But when the maskers enter, the pattern changes; the music goes down a third, from E flat to C, which inevitably sounds bright because it involves sharpening the previous key-note to E natural within the new tonic chord. The instrumentation serves to intensify the shock. There may be some irony in Giovanni's celebratory welcome, at his peasant party, to these noble strangers who are in fact his enemies, for the festive drums later become 'il tuon della vendetta' (13.11).

The second part of the finale goes the other way. With a conventional link of two bars in which Giovanni commands the dances to resume, it ascends to G, the dominant, and follows this sonata-like manoeuvre with another, the rapid modulations and deliberate illogicality of ending a section (13.9) on the dominant of D, but beginning the next one in F. There is a certain obvious symmetry, in the use of modulations falling a fifth as far as E flat, then rising a fifth (C to G, F to C). But the asymmetry is more important, and is created by the abrupt shift from E flat to C, with its reminder of the tonic sound, and the only passage of tonal instability (13.9), a break in musical decorum exactly matching the action.[11]

It is one thing to lead the ear from one key to the next within a continuous finale; another to expect a listener to appreciate the return of a tonality in pieces widely dispersed throughout the opera, separated by recitative (or dialogue), other numbers, or an entr'acte. No composer can reasonably expect to make a dramatic or musical point in this way unless the stages are marked by the return of characteristic melodies and instrumentation. Mozart cared enough about tonality to end all his mature operas in the key in which they began, which was by no means a generally followed convention. Yet only in *Don Giovanni* does he supply clear 'collateral' evidence to connect the tonality of the Over-ture with the last finale (No. 24). The connection is reinforced by taking in the whole opening sequence as far as the end of No. 2 (see Table 4). But for the major chords ending No. 24.6, both columns of Table 4 suggest closed forms in D minor. The finale, of course, con-cludes in D major, with the *scena ultima* (G, allegro, larghetto, ending on the dominant of D (24.8); D (24.9)). *Don Giovanni* thus does not end in exactly its original tonal condition, but with a move from D minor to D major which, unlike that of Overture, is not frustrated. The symmetries are obvious: the use of the same subsidiary keys, B flat and F for whole sections, G and A within sections (except for 24.8 where G

Table 4. *Parallel of opening and closing sequences*

		Key	Key		
Overture	Statue	d	D		24.1
	Allegro	D	D	Table-music	24.2a
		V/F			
		[A:G, g, B♭]			
No. 1	Leporello	F	F		24.2b
			B♭		24.2c
	Anna	B♭	B♭	Elvira	24.3
	Commenda-	[g–d–f–V/c]	V/d		
	tore		F	Leporello	24.4
No. 2	Recitative				
	Duet	d	d	Statue	24.5
			[a:b♭–g:d]		
			d–D	Allegro	24.6

is the tonic); the mixed mode of the tonic; and the direct association of the statue music. F belongs to Leporello, B flat to the distressed ladies; all the major keys participate in the *buffo* atmosphere which prevails until the two entries of the Commendatore, in flesh and in stone. Here at least a long-range tonal relationship is energetically exploited by the composer.[12] Its chief impact, however, is derived not from the keys as such, but from the dramatic parallelism of *buffo* scenes interrupted by momentous, even tragical, events; the corresponding musical styles and fluidity of forms; and details of musical invention which go beyond the obvious element of reprise.

The transmutation, in the first tableau of *Don Giovanni*, of a rough and farcical scene from the fair theatre into a species of musical drama unprecedented in force and continuity, is the sort of miracle of which only Mozart was capable. Even the entry of Anna and Giovanni is composed in a tone essentially belonging to *opera buffa*, despite its Gluckian use of regular, biting *sforzandi*; neither Gluck nor *opera seria* provided any precedent. It has often been noted, moreover, that the first few bars of Anna's music bear a close, if fortuitous, resemblance to Gazzaniga's handling of the same situation.[13] The action may be in deadly earnest; the musical setting is not, and the orchestra seems most concerned to support Leporello's anxious patter, leaving the others on their own, with Giovanni characteristically taking his tone from Anna (see Ex. 6C).

The musical form retains the sort of design used for 'Notte e giorno faticar', avoiding modulation and active sonata patterns. The music falls into repetitive groups, interlocking strophes (see Table 5). Open-ended

Table 5. *'Notte e giorno faticar' (No. 1, bars 1ff)*

Section	A1	A2	B1–B2	C (A3)	B1–B2	D	B2
Number of bars	10	9	13	12	13	6	7
Text	(Orch- estra)	Notte e giorno	Voglio e non voglio	O che caro	Repeat	Ma mi par	Non mi voglio
Key	F–V	F–V	F, close	F–V	F, close	[IV]	F, close

strophes (A, C) alternate with closed, cadences ones (B). C is really a new tune; D is a frightened mutter, with a new anapest rhythm ♪♪♩ which becomes Anna's upbeat: 'Non sperar'; the subdominant, unexpected B flat chords, becomes the next key. Leporello then completes his musical form with B2 to new words, a parallel invited by the text, however, and not perfunctory (it also shows that his desire to hide at the sound of danger is as strong as his desire to be a gentleman).

Similar structural principles are used in the next section, which is equally faithful to the key of B flat (see Table 6).

Table 6. *'Non sperar, se non m'uccidi' (No. 1, bars 73ff)*

Section	A1	A2	B1	B2	C1	C3	B2	C1	C2
Number of bars	5	5	7	8	4	10	4	4	15
Character(s)	A	G	a3	A, G	L	A, G; a3	A, G	L	A, G; a3
Key	B♭	B♭	B♭–V	V	V	B♭, close	V	V	B♭, close.

A: Anna; G: Giovanni; L: Leporello

The second B2 is the last four bars of the first; the second C2, after fourteen repeated bars, extends and reinforces the cadence. Anna and Giovanni are struggling, she to reveal his face, he to remain disguised (thus he cannot exert much force). The situation does not need Leporello's comments to be farcical, and it is not improper in production to use the musical repetitions for a repeated stage-picture of grimly humorous effect. Indeed the firm, static musical design directly contradicts typical descriptions of the scene, such as Noske's – 'A sequence of unusual and exciting events presented in a breathtaking dramatic rhythm.'[14] In fact Anna takes so long to get help, and Giovanni has so much time in which he might escape, that there is an immediate and undeniable problem for the producer interested in verisimilitude. Music, for Mozart, had inalienable rights: 'Passions, however rough, must never be expressed so as to arouse disgust, and music must never give offence to the ear even in the most desperate situations', as he wrote to his father when composing *Die Entführung* (26 September 1781). Consequently his scene is more secure musically than Gazzaniga's, as well as more dramatic in detail. It does not move in a realistic continuum, but in the conventional jerks of *opera buffa*. This makes the change of tone when the Commendatore appears doubly effective (the change of mood without change of tempo recurs as Elvira sees the statue, No. 24.3). Mozart marks this critical point by important cross-references (however subconsciously made) to places of equivalent seriousness: No. 2 and the second finale. And to simple strophic designs succeed completely flexible shapes, like recitative, closely related to the pace of action; and an advanced musical syntax, especially in harmony. The confrontation and fight occupy some 40 bars out of 194 in No. 1, and are followed by the timeless moment of the dying trio (see Ex. 6).

The whole problem of this most problematic of Mozart's operas is epitomized in this opening scene. The thrust and continuity of the last stages of No. 1, and much of No. 2, make the reversion to discrete operatic forms harder to accept, although it is done with tact, by growing towards a formal duet in No. 2 and by making the first aria (No. 3) a trio. (Having too good an opening scene is a difficulty with other operas as well, such as Gluck's *Iphigénie* operas.) The movement from simple *buffo*, through lively elegance (Anna) and excitement (the fight) to a passage of breathtaking beauty, accompanies an action of such beastliness that only the heartless treatment of the fair theatre (like Punch and Judy) is really suited to it. Thus the Mozartian miracle contains the seed of his opera's undoing. Noske remarks that only when the curtain falls after No. 2 'for the first time in the opera we hear a closing cadence in the orchestra. The opening scenes have lasted only twelve minutes, little more than the duration of a sonata movement.'[15] There is of course no sonata structure spanning Nos. 1 and 2, and there are plenty of cadences; but they rarely sound final, and the unity of these scenes, like that of a sonata movement, resides partly in an extended tonal scheme, and partly in numerous small-scale continuities and delayed explanation of discontinuities which prevent any sense of premature closure. The symmetry of principal keys is obvious: Overture, D minor – D major; No. 1, F – B flat, F minor; No. 2, D minor (see Table 4). But the F sections do not balance, and if they did they would tend to confirm a unity in No. 1 at the expense of the whole complex. Mozart provides no obvious connection between the Overture and No. 2 to confirm the tonality, but he forges powerful links by concentrating, at critical points, on complex harmonic progressions whose recognition does not depend upon the listener's sense of absolute pitch. Naturally there result potent links with the statue scene as well, and with their support the parallels indicated in Table 4 become less superficial.

The harmonic progressions by which these scenes are connected are less concerned with the standard dissonance of the period, the diminished seventh (despite its elaborate use in the statue scene), than with the augmented sixth, an equally ambiguous chord because it can also function as the dominant seventh of another key (see Ex. 8D). Mozart

Ex. 8

8A Overture

8B No. 24 from bar 7 of *più stretto*

[continued
as Ex. 10 B]

8C No. 2: Anna: Padre mio, caro padre, padre amato ...

exploits this enharmonic relationship as fully as any composer of the time, giving both resolutions full play in the andante of the Overture (Ex. 8A). (In Ex. 8 'y' denotes the augmented sixth, 'x' the diminished seventh, 'N' and 'n' the flat supertonic or Neapolitan: cf. Ex. 5). The andante is partly repeated in No. 24, but with a significant difference: the reprise of bars 1-22 (No. 24, bars 433-52) is followed by a modulation, and bars 23-6 reappear in No. 24 in A minor, greatly extended (bars 462-9). The harmonic idea of the cadence (bars 27-30) is given prominence later in the finale, at the chilly handclasp, when the tempo quickens. This passage (Ex. 8B) goes from G minor (bars 520, 527) by stark tritone steps in the bass (cf. Ex. 8A, square brackets). A series of rising sixth chords (bar 533; cf. Overture, bar 23, but the scales are now violent baroque rushes in the bass) reaches a Neapolitan complex (bar 538), here emphasized by the use of E flat *minor*, but otherwise less directly related to D. This debouches chromatically through C minor back to G minor (bar 545). The last tremendous progression differs motivically and even harmonically (using 'x' not 'y') from the equivalent passage in the Overture (from bar 17), but the bass-line is uncannily exact, and seems to resolve what was formerly ambiguous by going direct to the D minor cadence. As if to rub the point in, 'y' is reiterated in the allegro which forms a coda to the scene, at 'foco, pien d'orror' (bar 562) and the demons' first entry (bar 565).

In most cases the chord 'y' has its expected resolution, onto the dominant of D minor. But the alternative by which it *is* the dominant of E flat links the Overture (bar 20) to No. 2. During No. 1 we are reminded of the chord at the Commendatore's entrance (bar 154; Ex. 6A) where it takes the music from G to D minor; and, transposed to F, at the end of the fight (bar 174; Ex. 6B). Right outside this complex, a dramatically poignant recollection of this occurs in the middle of

No. 10 when Anna refers to her father's blood (in F, bar 90) and calls for revenge (in D, bar 99). More poignant still, however, is the reverse resolution to E flat in No. 2, just before Anna loses consciousness (Ex. 8C); the 'y' chord is used, exactly as in the Overture, to go to the Neapolitan and then the dominant (bars 36, 42). Now comes a sudden break in musical syntax; instead of the expected A major chord (dominant of D minor) it is A minor, and *its* dominant, on the significant bass-note G sharp (bar 44). Anna has fallen; this is Ottavio's move to support her. That an E flat chord (bar 129) and a bass move G sharp – A (bar 133; 'x' chord) recur when Anna calls for vengeance is probably a subconscious connection, as the two elements are not juxtaposed; but it is still potent. Forceful play is made in the closing stages of the duet with both 'y' (bars 152, 188) and the Neapolitan (bar 220).

Here too another remarkable cross-relation arises. A chromatic moan accompanies the Commendatore's death (Ex. 9A). It hovers over unresolved harmony, leaving the end of No. 1 open; but this is not a clear move, like the end of the Overture, to the dominant of a new key, but to a dominant (of C minor) with no statement of that key to follow. This breathtaking moment is succeeded by the dry rattle of secco recitative, in which the bass-movement B–C resolves the dominant of C

Ex. 9A

Ex. 9B

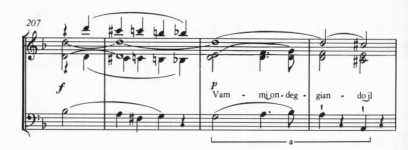

in the short term but, because it was left hanging by the orchestra, not at all in the longer term. The moment Anna sees the body, the same sixth on B violently initiates No. 2. At the end of No. 2 the chromatic figure recurs, accelerated but unmistakable (Ex. 9B); its third appearance is the end of No. 24.6, still faster (Ex. 9C). Thus the crime, the call to vengeance, and the fulfilment of vengeance, are linked; and the last two, in the same key, share a bass-figure of old-fashioned cut ('a' in Ex. 9B-C) and conclude with a vigorous anapest ('b'). These elements appear only in the codas of the movements and thus stand together by analogy. No. 2, however, closes a tonal cycle in D minor; No. 24.6 ends with the more decisive resolution onto D major, with plagal cadences, preparing for the prolonged plagal cadence of the *scena ultima* (in G then D). The latter is thus in a sense the resolution of the incomplete allegro of the

Overture, and appropriately enough in tonal terms, the coda to the whole opera.

The death-blow for the Commendatore was a powerful diminished seventh on B natural, leading to F minor (Ex. 6B). That same seventh, but with G sharp for A flat, brings him back from the dead. The mysteries of harmony, tremendous and beautiful, are Mozart's response to the tragic and supernatural elements of *Don Giovanni*. Although powerfully orchestrated and of a severe grandeur in rhythm, the scene is scarcely memorable for melody, even where the music dissolves into a unison. As the statue refuses mortal food his modulation from D to A minor seems to traverse the tonal universe (Ex. 10A); after going first

Ex. 9C

Ex. 10A

Ex. 10B

to G minor (harmonized), the line takes the simple step to an implied
E flat, but treats it as the Neapolitan of D, in which key C sharp stands
as dominant (cf. Ex. 8D). But the line avoids the expected D and rises
to F natural (cf. Ex. 5), only to refuse this resolution and plunge by a
tritone to a B natural, harmonized as part of the dominant of A. The
two phrases hang together as much by rhythmic correspondence as by
the harmonic chain they form, in which one link in the second phrase
barely holds. The unison cadence of the Commendatore's leave-taking
(Ex. 10B) is rich enough to serve, note for note, in one of Brahms'
most impassioned works, the B minor Rhapsody Op. 79 No. 1 (bars
14–16).

The scene as a whole is delineated by a sonata-like form, using the
same keys as the Overture but minor (see Table 4). In the Overture,

besides D and A, G and G minor are used at the false reprise (bar 141), and B flat is reached from G minor (it covers bars 151-60). In No. 24.5 the clearest tonal definitions are marked by the throbbing rhythm ('z' in Table 7), but the B flat minor section includes a last reprise of an idea from the Overture (bar 503; Overture bar 12) (see Table 7). Most

Table 7. *Statue scene No. 24.5*

Action	Entry		Rejection			Dialogue			Invitation			
Cross-references	Overture bars 1-11				Overture bar 23							
Bar	433	443	452 454 (Ex. 10A)		462	470	479	485	487	501	503	507
Character	Com.	G	Com.			L, G; Com.			Com.		L, G	Com.,
Motif	A (z)	B	(z)		C	(z) C	(z)			B		(z)
Key	d		bridge to a			a	cadence...		[bb]			...

Acceptance		Handclasp (*Più stretto*)			Exit (Allegro) 24.6
513 (Ex. 7)	517	521	527 (Ex. 8B)	549 (Ex. 10B)	554
G	Com., (z)	G (*Tremolo*)		Com.	
g			...d	cadence	d

Com.: Commendatore; G: Giovanni; L: Leporello
A, B and C are motifs from the Overture; z is the rhythm ♩. ♪ ♩. ♪
... indicates roving tonality

of the statue's speeches begin with a diminished seventh (the exception, bar 474 ('Parlo, ascolta, più tempo non hò'), uses a dominant seventh and augmented sixth). Bar 433 is the first full tutti with trombones; bar 452 ('Ferma un pò') ends the question of his supper (Ex. 10A); bar 487 begins his invitation by shattering the settled A minor; bars 508 and 511 are the single words 'Risolvi: Verrai?', with the voice falling a tenth (see Ex. 7). The music resolves to G minor; at bar 517 the statue gloomily joins the G minor chord, to release the *più stretto* with a diminished seventh as Giovanni takes his hand. All three possible diminished sevenths are used in these places in contexts so varied as to beggar description.

8 The literature of 'Don Giovanni'

The literature of *Don Giovanni* is so extensive that a small selection like what follows is bound to be arbitrary. Included here are two essential texts: the extracts relating to *Don Giovanni* from da Ponte's memoirs and the immensely influential interpretation of the opera by Hoffmann (for references to both see Index). I have also included a neat telling of the less improbable stories relating to the Prague première by Wilhelm Kühe. The review by Berlioz, not so far as I know previously translated into English, gives considerable insight into the condition of *Don Giovanni* at one time and place with, however, some claim to be representative for that epoch. Finally, I have included a bouquet of unusual tributes to the opera in music and literature.

A. Lorenzo da Ponte, *Memorie*

Maestri Martini, Mozzart [*sic*, passim], and Salieri, came to me all three at once to ask me for a drama. I liked and esteemed all three, and hoped to redeem past failures and with their help to add to my mite of theatrical glory. I pondered whether it might not be possible to satisfy all three of them by writing three operas at the same time. Salieri did not ask me to produce an original work. He had written the music for the opera *Tarare* in Paris, and now wanted it reshaped for the Italian style of drama and music; therefore he only asked me for a free translation. Mozart and Martín left it entirely to me to choose. For the former I chose *Don Giovanni*, a subject which pleased him very much, and for Martín, *L'arbore di Diana*, since for him I wanted a delicate subject suited to the sweetness of his melodies, which penetrate our souls, but which none knows how to imitate. Having found these three subjects, I went to the Emperor, told him of my ideas, and informed him of my intention to write these three operas simultaneously. 'You'll never manage!' he riposted. 'Perhaps not,' I answered, 'but I shall try. At night I shall write for Mozart, pretending that I am reading Dante's

Inferno – in the morning I shall write for Martín, and seem to be studying Petrarch. The evening will be for Salieri, and he will be my Tasso.' He
thought my parallel rather elegant, and as soon as I reached home I
began to write. I went to my desk and stayed there for twelve hours on
end. A little bottle of Tokay on my right, an inkpot in the middle, and
a pouch of Seville tobacco on my left. A lovely girl of sixteen whom I
should have liked to love only as a daughter, but – – was staying in
the house with her mother, who acted as housekeeper; she came to my
room at the sound of my bell, which in truth I rang pretty often, and
especially when my inspiration threatened to cool . . .

Meanwhile, on the first day, between the Tokay, the Seville tobacco,
the coffee, the bell and the young Muse, I wrote the first two scenes of
Don Giovanni, then two scenes of *L'arbore di Diana*, then more than
half the first act of *Tarare*, a title which I changed to *Axur*. I took these
scenes next morning to the three composers, who could scarcely believe
possible what they could read with their own eyes; and in sixty-three
days the first two operas were quite ready, and nearly two thirds of the
last. *L'arbore di Diana* was the first performed. It was very well received,
scarcely less so than *Una cosa rara* . . .

After only one performance of [*L'arbore di Diana*] I was obliged to
go to Prague, where the first performance of Mozart's *Don Giovanni*
was to take place at the arrival of the Princess of Tuscany in that city.
There I stayed only a week to direct the actors who were playing in it,
but before it was performed I was obliged to return to Vienna because
of an urgent letter received from Salieri in which, truthfully or otherwise, he told me that *Axur* was to be staged immediately for Franz's
wedding and that the Emperor had ordered him to summon me back . . .

I had not seen the performance of *Don Giovanni* at Prague, but
Mozart informed me at once of its wonderful reception, and Guardasoni
wrote to me as follows: 'Long live da Ponte! long live Mozart! all
impresarii, all performers ought to bless them. As long as you live,
poverty will scarcely be known in the theatre.' The Emperor summoned
me, and showering me with gracious words of praise made me a gift of
another hundred sequins, and told me how very much he wanted to see
Don Giovanni. Mozart returned and promptly gave the score to the
copyist, who hastened to copy out the parts, since Joseph had to go
away. It was produced – – and need I say it? *DON GIOVANNI* DID
NOT PLEASE. Everyone except Mozart was sure it lacked something
or other. So a few additions were made, a few arias were changed, and
again we exposed it on stage – And *Don Giovanni* did not please. And
what did the Emperor have to say about it? 'The opera is divine: it is

quite probably even lovelier than *Figaro*, but it is no meat for the teeth of my Viennese.' I relayed this saying to Mozart, who answered without upsetting himself 'Let us give them time to chew on it.' He was right. On his advice, I contrived to have the opera repeated frequently. At each performance the applause grew and bit by bit even the gentlefolk of Vienna with their bad teeth could enjoy its savour and appreciate its beauty, and considered *Don Giovanni* one of the loveliest operas to be performed in any theatre.

> Lorenzo da Ponte, *Memorie*, trans. from the Italian text, see Deutsch, *Mozart. Die Dokumente seines Lebens*, Kassel, 1961, 468-70.

I have omitted a description of the charms of his Muse; an account of the subject of *L'arbore di Diana*, the only wholly original libretto of the three; and a tale of how da Ponte's fee for *Don Giovanni* (50 sequins) was nearly stolen on his way back to Vienna. Doubt has been cast on his story because *Tarare,* Salieri's opera to an original libretto by Beaumarchais, was only performed on 8 June 1787. But it was probably completed well before; the Paris Opéra was not in the habit of mounting productions so swiftly as the Italian company in Vienna (see above, p.3). Salieri could have given the libretto to da Ponte well before the performance, in the spring of 1787. *L'arbore di Diana* was performed on 1 October 1787, *Don Giovanni* on 29 October, and *Axur, re d'Ormus* on 8 January 1788, which gives some support for da Ponte's doubts as to Salieri's truthfulness.

Wilhelm Kühe, *Recollections*

My father's house was the centre of artistic life in Prague. Under its roof, week by week, met actors, singers, and orchestral players. Chief among the latter I remember a tall gaunt elderly man, by name Wenzel Swoboda, a performer on the double-bass at the Opera House. He had been a member of the orchestra on the occasion of the production (October 29, 1787) of *Don Giovanni*, which was specially written by Mozart for the Prague Opera House, the master coming from Vienna to finish his work and conduct its first performance. . .The conceit (as I may term it) of the good people of my native city was increased a hundred-fold when Mozart, in a speech delivered at a banquet in his honour, declared (so Swoboda told me) that the citizens of Prague were the only people in the world who understood his music. Had he lived longer he might have modified this opinion. Speaking of Mozart, I am reminded that my friend Swoboda used also to refer to the pleasure evinced daily by the great master in the game of billiards. He would also from time to time recall Mozart's habit of laying aside mere speech in favour of musical recitative, which even in public he would use as

a means of making remarks and conveying requests to his circle of
friends. From the same authority I learned the positive truth of the
story (often told and as frequently denied) that on the night before its
production the overture to *Don Giovanni* had not even been sketched.
The impresario, said Swoboda, was in despair. Mozart's wife, however,
undertook that the overture should be finished in time. She accordingly
sat up all night with her husband, although she found it difficult to
keep him awake. As he wrote, the sheets of the score were passed from
his desk to those of a little army of copyists who were in attendance to
transcribe the instrumental parts. Again and again was the great maestro
overpowered by sleep, and every time he was aroused by his vigilant
helpmate he broke into song as follows:

These two bars continually recurred to him, and were as often written
down.

The ink, Swoboda recalled, was hardly dry on some of the pages
when they were placed on the desks of the orchestra. A rehearsal was
impossible. Nevertheless, the overture was played with a spirit which
not only roused the enthusiasm of the audience to the highest pitch,
but so greatly delighted the illustrious composer that, turning to the
orchestra, he exclaimed 'Bravo, bravo, Meine Herren, das war ausgezei-
chnet!' (Bravo, bravo, gentlemen, that was admirable!). At the end of
that memorable first night Mozart declared that such a performance at
sight was an extraordinary feat, 'obschon manche Noten unter die
Pulte gefallen sind' (although several notes had tumbled under the
desks).

And now another of Swoboda's reminiscences: At the final rehearsal
of the opera Mozart was not at all satisfied with the efforts of a young
and very pretty girl, the possessor of a voice of greater purity than
power, to whom the part of Zerlina had been allotted. The reader will
remember that Zerlina, frightened at Don Giovanni's too pronounced
love-making, cries for assistance behind the scenes. In spite of continued

repetitions, Mozart was unable to infuse sufficient force into the poor girl's screams, until at last, losing all patience, he clambered from the conductor's desk on to the boards. At that period neither gas nor electric light lent facility to stage mechanism. A few tallow candles dimly glimmered among the desks of the musicians, but over the stage and the rest of the house almost utter darkness reigned. Mozart's sudden appearance on the stage was therefore not noticed, much less suspected, by poor Zerlina, who at the moment when she ought to have uttered the cry received from the composer a sharp pinch on the arm, emitting, in consequence, a shriek which caused him to exclaim: 'Admirable! Mind you scream like that tonight!'

The opera as at first written did not terminate with the carrying off of Don Giovanni by the Furies. This episode was followed by four additional numbers, including a quartette by Donna Anna, Elvira, Zerlina, and Ottavio. After the first night, however, these pieces remained unheard until the jubilee performance of the opera at Prague in 1837, on which occasion I was present. They were then voted exceedingly dull, but it must be confessed that the whole representation was distinctly second-rate in the absence of several of the principal vocalists, who were down with *la grippe*. At the century performance, fifty years later, my brother travelled from Kieff to Prague on purpose to be present, my own intention of meeting him being frustrated by professional duties at home.

My friend Swoboda would sometimes refer to the consternation excited in Prague by the news of Mozart's death, in December, 1791, and would dwell on the solemnity of the *Requiem* Mass in the great church of St Nicholas (now disused), to which thousands vainly sought to gain admission.

Wilhelm Kühe, My Musical Recollections, London, 1896, 6-11

Wilhelm Kühe was born in Prague in 1823. A pupil of Tomašek, he made a career as a minor composer and travelling pianist, but settled in England in 1847. He organized a Brighton festival in the 1870s, and later taught at the Royal Academy of Music. What is original in his account of *Don Giovanni* is its claim to come from a first-hand witness, Swoboda, who, however, might well belong in the category of 'improvers' for the sake of the tale. The omission of the *scena ultima* after one night only is an unusual detail; it may well be incorrect, but it is indicative of the nineteenth century's attitude to the scene.

E. T. A. Hoffmann, 'Don Juan'

The special qualities of *Don Giovanni* were early perceived, or distorted, by the Romantic genius in literature. Goethe was keenly alive to its demonic element, and concluded that Mozart alone could have composed *Faust*, for which 'the music should be in the manner of *Don Giovanni*'.[1] E. T. A. Hoffmann's short story is introduced and concluded with a light ironic tone but turns into a fantastical and profound study of the implications of one aspect of the opera; in this blend of tones it resembles the work itself.

[The author presents himself (or his *alter ego*; for he addresses himself to 'mein Theodor', his own name) as a travelling composer and genuine connoisseur; the vignettes of philistine opera-goers are most amusing. He stays in a hotel and, on enquiring about the sounds of an orchestra that he hears, learns that his room opens into a box in the theatre. *Don Giovanni* is (most unusually) being given by a travelling Italian company in the original language. He describes the performance; in the middle of the first act he feels himself no longer alone and senses a woman in the box. At the interval he turns to her; is it Anna, or is it the *prima donna*? she talks pure Tuscan; she has sung one of the author's operas. She speaks of her role, how it engulfs her as she plays it. As the second act begins she clutches her heart and saying 'Unhappy Anna, now comes the most dreadful moment of all', she disappears. She plays the second act like one possessed, and looks near to death at the end. The author concludes his evening by writing about his adventure to 'Theodor'.[2]]

I felt so oppressed in my stuffy room! – About midnight I thought I heard your voice, my Theodor! you uttered my name clearly and rustling came from the tapestry-covered door. What was to stop me from visiting again the place of my wonderful adventure? – Perhaps I might see you, and she who fills my whole Being! How easy it would be to carry the little table – two lights – writing materials! The waiter looks for me with the punch I ordered; he finds the room empty, the tapestry door swung back: he follows me into the box and peers at me doubtfully. On my nodding, he puts down the drink on the table and goes off, looking me over again with a question on the tip of his tongue. I turn my back on him and lean over the rim of the box, gazing into the empty house whose architecture, magically illuminated by my two lights, appears strange and fairy-like as if it were marvellously reflected. A draught cutting through the house makes the curtain stir. – What if it were to rise? what if Donna Anna were to appear, frightened by terrible spirits? – 'Donna Anna!' I cry involuntarily: the cry echoes in the empty house, but the ghosts of the orchestral instruments wake to it – a mysterious sound shivers up; it seems to contain a whisper of the beloved name! – I cannot repress a secret shudder, but it thrills through my nerves delectably.

I master my feelings and become calm enough, my Theodor! at least to impart to you how, for the first time, I believe I understand the most noble work of the divine master in all its characteristic depths. – Only a poet can understand a poet; only a Romantic feeling can penetrate the Romantic; only a poetically exalted spirit, who partakes in the mystery of the Temple of Art, can understand what the initiated utters in his frenzy. – If you consider the poem (of *Don Giovanni*), without assuming any deeper meaning, taking into consideration only the events, you can hardly grasp how Mozart could imagine and compose such music for it. A *bon vivant* who loves wine and girls immoderately, who arrogantly invites the stone man, who portrays the old father whom he cut down in self-defence, to join him at his festive table – surely there is nothing very poetic in this, and it was honestly hardly worth the trouble taken by the subterranean powers to pick him out as a collector's item; or for the stone man, filled by a transfigured spirit, to get off his horse, in order to persuade the sinner to repentance at his last hour; or indeed for the devil to send his best troops to draw him along the most hideous road into his kingdom. – Believe me Theodor! Nature created Don Juan as the dearest child of her womb, raised in every way above the common round, above the manufactured, empty symbols, in themselves worthless and only to be valued by numbers as they pour from the workshop; raised him nearly to godhead, one fit to conquer, to command. A stronger, more handsome body, a form which exudes fire, and who kindles in his heart intimations of the highest; deep feelings, an agile understanding. – But the terrible result of man's fall into sin is that the devil still has the power to corrupt and to turn his striving for the highest, which itself reveals the divine part of him, to evil ends. This conflict between godly and demonic powers embodies the idea of earthly life, just as a difficult victory gives us an idea of the heavenly. Don Juan was raised up by the demands life makes on such a mental and physical organization as his, and an eternally burning desire, from which his blood flowed boiling in his veins, drove him on so that he greedily and insatiably seized on every phenomenon of the physical world, vainly seeking for fulfilment! – There is nothing on earth which so uplifts the innermost nature of a man as Love; it is love which, working in secrecy and strength, either destroys or illuminates the depths of our being; so can we wonder that Don Juan hoped to still the longings which tore at his heart through love, and that the devil through love was able to slip a rope round his neck? The cunning of the old enemy planted in Don Juan's mind the idea that love, through the pleasuring of women, could fulfil for him on earth what dwells in our hearts as no more than a promise of Heaven, and is that unquenchable longing which brings us into some understanding of the heavenly. Restlessly fleeing from lovely women to lovelier; enjoying their delights with glowing ardour to the point of satiety, of destructive drunkenness; always thinking himself deceived in his choice, always hoping to find ultimate gratification in an Ideal, Juan was bound at the end to find everything on earth dull and superficial and, since he had come utterly to despise mankind, he turned against the delusion which he had thought the highest that life could offer, but which had trapped him so sharply. No delight of womankind now brought gratification to his senses, but only increased his rancour and mockery against Nature and the Creator. Deep despite for the ordinary things in life, which he considered himself above, and bitter scorn for men, who in the happiness of love could expect at least some fulfilment of the higher feelings which Nature has cruelly granted us through a homely and bourgeois union with one another, drove him to revolt against such institutions of Society and meditate their destruction wherever he found them, as part of his battle with the unknown Being, master of our fate, which seemed to him a mischievous monster indulging in cruel sport at the expense of the miserable beings it had created. − Every abduction of a beloved bride, every blow struck at the happiness of lovers to cause them eternal sorrow, became a noble victory over the enemy power, which raised him still further out of life's rut, above Nature, above the Creator! − He wills himself more and more away from life, but only to dive still further into Hell. The seduction of Anna, with its surrounding occurrences, is the highest point to which he has attained.

In the highest endowments of Nature, Donna Anna is the counterpart to Don Juan. Just as Don Juan was originally a wonderfully powerful and fine-looking man, so is she a divine woman, over whose pure spirit the devil is powerless. The arts of Hell can only overcome her earthly part. − Satan having once completed this conquest, Heaven has decreed that Hell can no longer avoid consummating its revenge. − The mocking Don Juan invites the murdered old man to a cheerful feast, and the enlightened spirit, who can now for the first time understand his adversary as a fallen being and can pity him, is prepared to come to him in awesome guise to warn him that he must repent. But so corrupted, so darkened is his mind, that no ray of hope from the heavenly blessing can penetrate his soul, and show him the way to a better existence! −

Certainly it will have struck you, my Theodor, that I have mentioned Anna's seduction; and, as well as I can at this hour when thoughts and ideas from the depths of my mind overcome words, I shall tell you briefly how the music, without regard to the text, illuminates for me the whole relationship between these two natures locked in conflict (Don Juan and Donna Anna). – I have already explained that Anna is the counterpart of Juan. What if Donna Anna was called down by Heaven so that Juan might learn to know through love the divine nature that dwelt in him, and which corrupted him through Satan's wiles; and to wrench him away from the annihilating struggle with despair? Too late; he saw her at the height of his criminal folly, and could only feel the demonic impulse to undo her. – She was not saved! when he rushed forth the deed was done. The fire of a superhuman sensuality, glowing from Hell, flowed through her innermost being and made her impotent to resist. Only he, only Don Juan, could arouse in her the lustful abandon with which she embraced him, he who sinned with the overpowering, destructive frenzy of the hellish spirit within him. When he, his will accomplished, wants to escape, her mind is seized with torturing pains by realization of her sin, which she sees as a hideous monster, spewing forth deadly poison. – Her father's death at Don Juan's hand, her engagement to the cold, unmanly, ordinary Don Ottavio, whom once she thought she loved – even the frenzied love which had filled her innermost self with a consuming flame, and which had flooded forth at the moment of highest ecstasy and now burns with a glow of annihilating hatred: all these things are tearing her asunder. She feels that only Don Juan's downfall can bring peace to the anxious torment of her soul; but this peace will be her own earthly downfall. – Therefore she incessantly urges her frigid bridegroom to revenge, she herself pursues the betrayer, and only when the underworld powers have dragged him down to Orcus does she become calmer – only she cannot submit to her bridegroom, eager for their wedding: 'lascia, o caro, un anno ancora, allo sfoga del mio cor!' She will not live out this year; Don Ottavio will never embrace her, whose pious spirit has saved her from remaining Satan's wedded bride.

How vitally I feel all this enter the depths of my soul with those heartrending chords of the first recitative and of the narrative of the nocturnal attack! – Even the scena for Donna Anna in the second act: 'crudele' [No. 23], which, superficially considered, is concerned only with Don Ottavio, speaks in secret harmonies, in the most wonderful progressions, in that inner voice of a soul sundered from all earthly happiness. What else can be meant, even if, for the poet, unconsciously, by the words of that astonishing closing section:

forse un giorno il cielo ancora sentirà pietà di me! –

It strikes two o'clock! – A warm electric sigh quivers over towards
me – I sense the soft caress of that fine Italian perfume, which yesterday made me aware for the first time of my companion. I am seized
with a blissful sensation which I believe I could only give expression to
in music. The wind blows more strongly through the theatre – the
strings on the grand piano in the orchestra rustle – Heavens! now I
seem to hear Anna's voice coming from a great distance, come gliding
on the wings of the sound of an ethereal orchestra: 'Non mi dir, bell'idol
mio!' – Fling wide your gates, O remote, unknown empire of spirits –
O Djinnistan full of glory, where an inexpressible, heavenly sorrow,
like an unspeakable joy, fills the enraptured soul beyond all measure
with joys unpromised on earth! Let me step into the circle of your
most blessed and lovely illusions! May the dream, which now stirs us
with terror, now is sent as a friendly messenger to mortal men – may it
carry my soul, when sleep holds my body in leaden bands, to Elysian
plains!

[In a brief conversation, which serves as epilogue, the author hears that
the singer, deeply affected by her role, had spent the interval of the
opera unconscious in her dressing-room (this was the time of their conversation); and that she had died at two o'clock that morning.]

'Don Juan, a Fabulous Happening which Befell a Travelling Enthusiast',
Fantasiestücke in Callots Manier, Bamberg, 1814; first published
in the *Allgemeine Musikalische Zeitung*, 31 March 1813

Berlioz, 'Don Juan'

The production staged at the Paris Opéra in 1834 (see above, p. 75)
was the subject of a substantial article by Berlioz, which, however, did
not appear until November 1835. At this time Berlioz, in his thirty-third
year and recently married to the Irish actress Harriet Smithson, was
establishing himself as one of the leading music critics of the French
capital – more, perhaps, than as its leading composer.

Yesterday evening *Don Giovanni* was given at the Opéra. I am not going
to analyse it: God forbid! Too many learned critics, musicians, poets,
or those who are both poet and musician (like Hoffmann) have held
forth on this huge subject, to the extent that there is nothing left for
the gleaner. I shall confine myself to a few general observations about
this astounding work, evergreen, ever-powerful, ever in the vanguard of
musical civilization, when so many others of less than half its age have
fallen, forgotten corpses in wayside ditches, or are already begging for
support in voices so broken as to be scarcely audible. When Mozart

wrote it, he was well aware that success for a work of this kind would
be slow to come, and that perhaps he would not live to see it. He often
said, speaking of *Don Giovanni*, 'I wrote it for myself and my friends.'[3]
He was right to expect nothing better than the admiration of the few
advanced musicians of his time; the evidence for this is the coldness of
the general public when confronted with the musical monument which
he had raised. Even if the greatness of Mozart is now generally admitted
in France, it is not because of any genuine understanding by the *dilet-
tanti*, but because of the influence on them exerted by the unwavering
approbation of distinguished artists of all nations – an opinion which
finally percolates through to the mind of the man in the street like a
religious dogma upon which controversy is not permitted, and which it
would be criminal to doubt. Nevertheless the success of *Don Giovanni*
at the Opéra, even if it is a financial success, may be regarded as showing
a distinct progress in the level of our musical education. It demonstrates
that, without being bored, a good many people can now enjoy music
which is profoundly considered, carefully composed, orchestrated with
taste and dignity, always expressive, dramatic, true; a music which is
free and proud, which does not defer to the groundlings, and which, to
adapt a phrase of Shakespeare's, holds dearer the approval of a few *high
minds than the plaudits of a roomful of vulgar spectators*. The number
of the initiated is even big enough today for a genius no longer to feel
compelled to spoil his work by cutting it down to the size of his audience. It is true that most habitual opera-goers are still blinkered in their
outlook; but their expectations are slowly being modified; disorientation
caused by the successive loss of their illusions is causing the stragglers
to side blindly with the ideas of those in the vanguard of progress, and
they regularly congratulate themselves on having followed the latter
along a path to such marvellous discoveries. Certain aspects of great
compositions will remain caviar to the general for some time to come,
but at least hieroglyphics are no longer considered meaningless and we
have ceased to despair of ever understanding them. People are beginning
to realize that there is *style* in music as well as in poetry; that basement
musicianship exists, as does literature of the antechamber; operas for
grisettes and soldiers, like novels for kitchen-maids and grooms. It is
gradually being deduced that it is not enough for a piece of music to
affect the ear agreeably; it should also fulfil other conditions, without
which music will never be raised much above the art of the fairground
and carnival. It will eventually even dawn on people that if it is absurd
to wish to exclude from the orchestra even the humblest of its instruments, since every one can be used to good effect if properly and care-

fully deployed, it is a hundred times more so to treat the orchestra as
if it were a piano with the sustaining-pedal permanently down; to hear
all the notes mixed up without distinguishing their function, disregarding
the melody which is swamped, the harmony which is blurred, the injury
to dramatic sense, or the offence to delicate ears. Obviously it is mon-
strous to greet the entry of Mlle Taglioni with a braying ophicleide and
a thunderous bass drum; such a barbarous combination, suitable for the
lumbering of a cyclops, would be ludicrous as an accompaniment to
the dancing of that most graceful of sylphides. And it would be just as
perturbing to hear a piccolo doubling the vocal bass three octaves up, or
a violin accompaniment *a punta d'arco*, enlivening a hymn sung by
priests bowed low before a tomb. Eventually the deplorable consequences of this fairground musical technique will be understood. How
on earth is it possible to produce powerful contrasts in this way? Where
can a thoughtful composer find the means to represent shades of
meaning, without which there simply *is* no music? Suppose that he
wants his orchestra to sound terrifying, imposing, appalling; the trombones, the ophicleide, the trumpets and horns are ready, he sets them
going . . . but of course they produce nothing like the intended effect,
and the audience is neither frightened nor awed by this mass of brass.
We hear the same racket every day accompanying a love-duet or epitha-
lamium; we are used to it, and the impact on which the composer was
banking misfires since his means are nothing unusual. If, on the other
hand, the composer needs gentle and delicate instrumentation, or at
least wants to convey something more subtly than by seizing the audience by the throat, we can be sure that nobody will pay sufficient attention to appreciate it, since they are used to hearing dialogue buried
by a raving orchestra. This is why I think that before we knew *Robert
le diable* and the second act of *Guillaume Tell*, it would have been
madness to expect much success for a score such as *Don Giovanni* at
the Opéra. Public appetite was gorged; and we owe our perception of
the art of effective usage of the orchestra's riches to the beneficient
effect of these two exemplary works. So at last Mozart comes into his
own.

   It is a pity that it was considered necessary to take various dances,
extended, lopped off, reordered, and orchestrated according to the
method which seems to me so inimical to musical sense and the interests
of art, from other works of Mozart, and insert them into *Don Giovanni*;
without these additions the absolutely pure style of this sublime score,
boldly breaking the public habits of the last eight or ten years, might
have completed this important revolution. And do not forget that

Mozart alone should receive the credit for such an attempt. No one has yet had the nerve to say that *his* orchestration is thin or his melodic style superannuated; his name has retained all its prestige, with the knowledgeable and ignorant, young composers and old masters, alike. So it is possible to mount this work which as a whole and in details is a cutting indictment of the methods of one modern school of composition, without fear of being attacked for resurrecting a museumpiece. Such an attempt, on the other hand, would have been very unwise with a new work. All around we should have heard that the music was faded, the orchestration skimpy, and devoid of brilliance and energy; simply because the bass drum does not feel compelled to let fly in every movement, backed by side-drum, a pair of timpani, cymbals, and triangle, and accompanied by a glittering cohort of brass. Imbeciles! do you not know that Weber never permitted the bass drum in his orchestra; that Beethoven, whose power you will not, I hope, deny, used it only once; and that in *The Barber of Seville* and some other of Rossini's works it does not play a single note! So if the whole orchestra seems feeble and skimpy to you when deprived of this cumbersome auxiliary, blame those whose abuse of violence has made you insensitive, and listen more carefully to a composer who, because he only employed *noise* on a few exceptional occasions, is the most far-seeing about the real sources of his art's power.

This is how we now welcome Mozart, as is shown by the religious silence with which we listen at the Opéra to the statue scene; his entry at the Théâtre Italien is usually the signal for the place to empty. No question here of a *prima donna* or a honeyed tenor giving a singing-lesson to the dandies of the dress circle; no question of a duet *à la mode* in which two stars compete in skill and inventiveness; it is only dirge-like singing, a sort of recitative, but sublime in its truth and grandeur. And as the orchestration of the preceding scenes was discreet and moderate, it follows that at the apparition of the ghost, the trombones, which have been silent for some time, send a chill of terror through one, and a simple drumstroke, beaten intermittently beneath menacing harmonies, suffices to grip the entire audience. This scene is so extraordinary, and the composer has invented such miracles for it, that it always overwhelms the singer in the role of the Commendatore; one's imagination becomes excessively demanding and a unison of ten Lablaches would hardly suffice to give utterance to such a speech. This problem does not arise with the anguished cries of Don Juan, struggling in the icy clutches of the marble colossus. As the wicked seducer of Donna Anna is after all only human, the imagination only requires human sounds from him, and this, of all passages in his varied role, is the one the actor usually brings off best. At least it seems so to me with Garcia, Nourrit, and Tamburini.

The role of Ottavio has become almost taboo because the perfection with which Rubini sings the famous aria 'Il mio tesoro' is enough to reduce his rivals to despair. I name only this aria because there is no point in pretending that he sings the rest of the part nearly as well. In the ensembles, like the first-act duet [No. 2], Rubini seems to try to efface himself completely; the many passages at the lower end, or even in the middle, of his range evidently obstruct the full flowering of this wonderful voice, which seems made to soar above the others rather than accompany them. Consequently this duet normally makes a far greater impact at the Opéra than at the Théâtre Italien. It should be added at once that much of this difference derives from Mlle Falcon. Mlle Grisi hardly likes Mozart, and plays Donna Anna with an ill grace; since in Italy *Don Giovanni* has never been granted full rights of citizenship, she could not learn to enjoy such music there. Mlle Falcon, however, sings the part with love, even passion; the feelings which torment her emerge as a trembling of the voice in certain touching passages, as vehemence when certain notes are flung out; she employs all her skill to illumine various corners of the picture that most of her rivals are content to leave in shadow. I have never heard Mlle Sontag sing Donna Anna, but of all the others I have seen undertaking this difficult role, Mlle Falcon seems to me undoubtedly the best in every respect. I would only take issue with her on the way in which she delivers certain passages of diatonic *gruppetti* where the notes are slurred together in pairs, like those in the duet with Ottavio in Act I [No. 2, bars 189ff]. Mlle Falcon here accentuates the first note of each pair so strongly that the second is almost inaudible; from a distance this unevenness sounds quite different from what the singer probably intends, resulting in an effect comparable to the phrasing of horns when they use open and stopped notes in alternation. Delivered like this, the passage I refer to in the *Don Giovanni* duet loses much of its proper force. Unless this were pointed out Mlle Falcon would never be able to notice it, since the effect is quite different from near by.

I cannot pass over in silence the electrifying reading of the grand finale in the first performance. The care taken with the general rehearsals, and the confidence acquired by every member of the chorus through minute and carefully directed study, are not the only reasons for this result. Every actor at the Opéra who had no role in this work had asked to take part in the chorus in this finale, so that the unusual increase in numbers, and the vigorous performance of these additional singers and their genuine enthusiasm (which was transmitted to the rest), were factors uniting to make the passage a real prodigy of choral performance even for the Opéra. As, moreover, Mozart's orchestra, despite all its richness and strength, never drowns the singers, we were for once able to hear what such a chorus can be like when it is properly performed. There's real dramatic music!!!

Journal des Débats, 15 November 1835, reprinted in Berlioz,
Les musiciens et la musique, 3-13

Although the performance was praised for its comparative 'authenticity' it is not only the inserted dances that qualify this view, but the tell-tale references to the chorus and, perhaps, the trombones, which should not have been heard at all except in the graveyard scene: Berlioz's reference suggests that they were included in earlier tuttis. Of the singers mentioned, Lablache, Tamburini, Rubini, and Grisi were in the cast at the Théâtre Italien in this period; Lablache was noted for the power of his bass voice. The performance under review included Nourrit, Falcon, and Levasseur (Leporello, another deep and powerful bass). We note that the Elviras, as well as Zerlinas, Masettos, and Commendatores, are not named. Besides Henrietta Sontag Berlioz might have mentioned among famous Annas of the time Wilhemine Schröder-Devrient, who probably contributed more than any to the Romantic dramatization *alla* Hoffmann (see Bitter, *Wandlungen*, 99). Garcia preceded Tamburini at the Théâtre Italien.

Certain tributes to Mozart's *Don Giovanni* take a purely musical form. There were the usual eighteenth-century arrangements for wind instruments, and the young Beethoven wrote variations for two oboes and cor anglais on 'Là ci darem' (1797, WoO 28). Much later he turned 'Notte e giorno faticar' into No. 22 of his Diabelli variations, a wry joke at the publisher's expense. 'Là ci darem' was used by Chopin in variations for piano and orchestra Op. 2 (1827), the work which Schumann greeted with 'Hats off!' and which for him directly evoked Seville: 'Surely that was Leporello winking at me, and Don Juan flying past in his white cloak.'[4] Sigismond Thalberg wrote two fantasies, one ' . . . sur la sérénade et le menuet de Don Juan' Op. 42, in which these most artless numbers consort strangely with his characteristically empty virtuosity, and one with variations, Op. 14. Liszt's 'Don Juan' fantasy (1841), however, is a feverishly inventive 'recreation' using the statue music, 'Là ci darem' with variations, and 'Fin ch'an dal vino', the last two ingeniously combined with fragments of the first.

Other composers have paid similar tributes, as has that most musical of writers, James Joyce, in *Ulysses*. Although Leopold Bloom refers to 'light opera of the Don Giovanni description' (p. 582)[5] its music haunts him deeply, even if this appears most in his puzzling over the words (for his Italian is weak). The statue music occurs to him in the 'Lestrygonians' (p. 179) as he leaves his own *cena*: 'What does that *teco* mean? Tonight, perhaps.' This moment is recalled among the distortions of 'Circe' (p. 466). But it is 'Là ci darem' which follows Mr Bloom around, entwined with thoughts of his own faithless Penelope and her lover, who are proposing to perform it together – in more than one sense. Curiously, and significantly, he misquotes the half-acceptance of Zerlina, substituting 'voglio' for the first 'vorrei' in 'Vorrei e non vorrei, Mi trema un poco il cor'; and at the first appearance of this motif in his thoughts ('Calypso', pp. 65–6) and later in the heat of business ('Aeolus', p. 122) he worries about the pronunciation of the non-existent 'voglio'. In 'The Lotus-Eaters' (p. 78) it drifts into his thoughts through the word 'will':

Curious the life of drifting cabbies, all weathers, all places, time or setdown, no will of their own. *Voglio e non.* Like to give them an odd cigarette. Sociable. Shout a few flying syllables as they pass. He hummed:

> *Là ci darem la mano*
> La la lala la la.

But when in 'Hades' he suddenly thinks of his wife, he corrects himself:

And *Madame.* Twenty past eleven. Up. Mrs Fleming is to clean. Doing her hair, humming: *voglio e non vorrei.* No: *vorrei e non.* Looking at the tips of her hairs to see if they are split. *Mi trema un poco il.* Beautiful on the *tre* her voice is: weeping tone. A thrust. A throstle. There is a word throstle that expressed that. (p. 95)

This is a touching moment, a clear affectionate vision from the graveyard. Thus *Don Giovanni* obsesses not only musicians, philosophers, and psychologists, but one of the completest 'heroes' of English literature as he muses through Bloomsday, among other things, on amorous episodes of his own.

Notes

1 Introduction

1. Mozart's letters are identified by date, and citations are translated from Deutsch, *Mozart: Briefe*; full English texts are in Anderson, *Letters of Mozart*, except for 29 September 1787.
2. Mozart's autograph is in the Bibliothèque Nationale, Paris; a facsimile has been published, ed. Lesure. Details of its contents and full lists of sources are in Köchel, 6th edn., and the Neue Mozart Ausgabe score, ed. Plath and Rehm.
3. Common errors about the genesis of *Don Giovanni* can be corrected by examination of the preliminary libretto, almost certainly prepared for the censor in Vienna in the summer of 1787 (it bears on the title-page the intended date of the first performance, 14 October, and the occasion, 'the arrival of Her Royal Highness Maria Theresia'). The libretto is significantly incomplete (see Einstein, 'The First Libretto'); besides much of the first act and the end of the second finale, it lacks the references to music played during the supper scene, as indeed does the Prague libretto. Common errors are the statement that Act II was intended to begin with recitative (the libretto shows it as a duet, with parts of the text to be sung 'a 2'), and that the graveyard scene had no recitative, and consisted only of the duet No. 22 (the libretto has the recitative text entire – although, curiously enough, this recitative is missing from Mozart's autograph).

   The shortest list of what was certainly composed in Prague (Overture, and Nos. 6, 14, and 24) is that of Köchel. To these the Neue Mozart Ausgabe adds Nos. 5 and 16, but with queries. No. 5, however, appears to be written on larger paper. Lesure, in the Introduction to the facsimile, points out that the following are on smaller paper: Overture, and Nos. 6, 14, 16, 17, 22, and 24. To these some recitatives should be added. Tiersot (*Don Juan*, 140-1) reached the same conclusion, and the facsimile (for what its evidence is worth) supports this. The possibility cannot be excluded, therefore, that all these were written in Prague.

   The first Giovanni, Bassi, later made the impossible claim that Mozart rewrote 'Là ci darem' (No. 7) five times to please him; but Mozart would never have tampered with an ensemble to suit a singer (see Jahn, *Life of Mozart*, III, 130; Jahn's statement that 'Là ci darem' is on smaller paper is an error). Conceivably the story may be true of No. 16 or 17.

4. One may accuse those who choose the last night of making a better story, but those who choose the penultimate night of shielding Mozart from a charge of gross irresponsibility. See p.124; and for a comprehensive sifting of tales, Procházka, *Mozart in Prag*, 92-115. Niemetschek gives the last night (*Life of Mozart*, 63-4); he was in Prague in 1787, but may be copying from the *Nekrolog auf das Jahr 1791* (Gotha, 1793) of Friedrich Schlichtegroll. His source was Constanze, but her second husband, Nissen, in his *Biographie W. A. Mozarts*, makes it the penultimate night. Forty years after the event 'Madame' (Constanze) confirmed to the Novellos 'the truth of her sitting up all night with him whilst he wrote the overture to "Don Giovanni" ' (Vincent and Mary Novello, *A Mozart Pilgrimage*, ed. R. Hughes (London, 1955), 95). Mozart's slightly wrong version of the opening in his personal catalogue could be interpreted either way; it does not prove that he had written the Overture down, as is sometimes claimed, by the twenty-eighth, only that he knew how it would begin, and the error is no evidence the other way since it does not correspond to the finale either, and that must have been written down long before (the bass minims, bars 2 and 4, appear as crotchets).

5. The *Mozart-Bibliographie* of Angermüller and Schneider gives fractionally more index-space to *Die Zauberflöte* than to *Don Giovanni*; they easily outstrip their rivals. However, Bernard Shaw is unaccountably missing, as are several philosophical and literary works pertaining directly to the Mozart version of Don Juan.

6. Fitzlyon, *The Libertine Librettist*, 141.

7. D. Heartz, 'The Creation of the buffo Finale in Italian Opera', *Proceedings of the Royal Musical Association* 104 (1977-8), 68. See also Noske, *The Signifier and the Signified*, 76-9. Elsewhere Heartz argues that Mozart must have picked the subject and Bertati as model. It would not be much to his credit; but there is really no reason to suppose that da Ponte, admittedly unreliable at times, lied in this case, since he cheerfully acknowledges Mozart's choice of *Figaro* (Heartz, 'Goldoni'). Gazzaniga's opera is nowadays often entitled *dramma giocoso*, even in Kunze's edition of the score; but not in his acknowledged sources, where it appears as *atto solo*, *farse giocose*, or, in da Ponte's adaptation played in London in 1794, 'tragi-comic opera' (a production with which Bertati clearly had no connection).

2 Synopsis

1. The political implications of 'Viva la libertà' were taken seriously enough by the Austrian censorship in the nineteenth century for it to be changed, in Italy, to 'Viva la società' (Petrobelli, 'Don Giovanni in Italia', 36). See also Rosen, *The Classical Style*, 94.

2. See S. Orlinck, 'A Canzonetta fiorentina in *Don Giovanni?*', *Mozart*

Jahrbuch (1967), 312. The melody appears in a collection which may, however, be late enough for it to be borrowed from Mozart. His bass is used, without its one chromatic note (a G sharp); the melody shows very small difference of ornamental detail. The possibility cannot be dismissed that da Ponte or Bassi might have given Mozart the tune, although the latter probably did not, since the text is in the preliminary libretto (Vienna, summer 1787). There are no obvious literary or operatic precedents for the serenade; a passing reference to it appears in a subliterary source (Biancolelli; see p. 32), where the servant says 'When my master has given his serenade and gone off, I say it is so dark I mustn't speak for fear of losing my words . . .'

3. The scene was put together by Mozart with his actors on the basis of operas popular in Prague (see p. 3). *Una cosa rara* was da Ponte's first major success as a librettist, and it briefly eclipsed *Figaro* in Vienna. It was given in Prague just before *Don Giovanni* (autumn 1787). Sarti's *I due litiganti* was a highly successful piece, first given in Milan in 1782 and known in Vienna and Prague from 1783.

4. The common nineteenth-century practice of omitting the *scena ultima* may have Mozart's authority. It is missing from the 1788 Vienna libretto, and Mozart composed a 'scream' for the women and Ottavio, a D major chord (bar 596, with Leporello). Masetto is not included, possibly because the characters were meant to run on; which for him, since he had played the Commendatore, would not be worth a change of costume. Mozart crossed this idea out (facsimile, Neue Mozart Ausgabe, Vorwort, xiii). There is also a way of abbreviating the scene entered by Mozart in the autograph. From the awestruck 'Ah! certo è l'ombra. . .' it goes directly to the moral: 'Resti dunque quel birbon.' Four bars of Andante were composed to replace bars 689-749. A Vienna score (not autograph) includes the *scena ultima*; the Florentine score, the source of certain recitatives peculiar to the Vienna version, omits it. In default of further evidence the chronology of these cuts must remain uncertain; possibly various ways of ending the opera were tried out during 1788. There is no way of knowing which the authors finally preferred.

3 Don Juan before da Ponte

1. Details of modern reprints and translations of literary texts, and of subliterary sources, are given in the Bibliography to this chapter. Synopses of literary and operatic forms are found in the Mozart literature, notably Jahn, *Life of Mozart*, III, 146ff (Tirso, Giliberto, Goldoni, Gluck's ballet, Righini's opera, Bertati); Dent, *Mozart's Operas*, 1st edn, 192ff (Bertati, 201ff); 2nd edn, 120ff (Goldoni is added, 123ff; Bertati, 129ff); Newman, *More Opera Nights* (very detailed synopsis of Tirso, 300-9; Dumas, *Don Juan de Marana*, 312). See also Kunze, *Don Giovanni vor Mozart*.

2. Jean-Auguste Julien Desboulmiers, *Histoire anecdotique et raison-née du Théâtre Italien* (Paris, 1769), I, 85-94.
3. Rousset, *Le mythe de Don Juan*, 136.
4. An Italian play by Onofrio Giliberto (1652) has been lost but some details survive (see above, n. 1). It was probably more serious than Cicognini's, and it was the direct source for two French tragicom-edies which preceded Molière's play, and which explored some of the moral and social implications (Dorimond, 1658, and de Villiers, 1659, both entitled *Le festin de pierre ou Le fils criminel*). After Molière came Rosimond's *Nouveau festin de pierre* (1669) which with Dorimond's play contributed to the brutal conception of Juan in the first English version, Shadwell's *The Libertine* (1776). None of these dramas is likely to have been known to either Bertati or da Ponte.
5. The Neapolitan MS already quoted (above, p. 28), and one from the Biblioteca Casanatense, Rome, in Spaziani, *Don Giovanni.*
6. Salvator Rosa, letter to Giovan Battista Ricciardi, 25 January 1669, ed. Aldo de Rinaldis, *Lettere inedite di Salvator Rosa a Giovan Battista Ricciardi* (Rome, 1939), quoted by Macchia, *Vita di Don Giovanni*, 75 and 81.
7. *Mozart's Operas*, 2nd edn only, 125.

4 The libretto

1. Abert, *Mozart's Don Giovanni*, 40.
2. Bitter, *Wandlungen*, 17-24.
3. Jahn, *Life of Mozart*, III, 164; Abert, *Mozart's Don Giovanni*, 42; Dent, *Mozart's Operas*, 1st edn, 243; 2nd edn, 164.
4. Rosen, *The Classical Style*, 301.
5. The question of Casanova's involvement in the libretto of this scene can be quickly dismissed. The preliminary libretto printed in Vienna in the summer of 1787 includes the entire sequence virtually as Mozart set it – *before* going to Prague. Casanova did not write any of it. See Newman, *More Opera Nights*, 383-6, for a rehearsal of the question; Dent's speculations (*Mozart's Operas*, 2nd edn only, 141ff) are quite unfounded. Casanova did, for some unknown purpose, draft an alternative text for Leporello's escape (No. 20 or the Vienna recitative which replaced it) – not, as is often stated, for the sextet itself (facsimile in Buchner, *Mozart and Prague*, and Nettl, *Mozart in Böhmen*). See also Nettl, 'Don Gio-vanni und Casanova', *Mozart Jahrbuch* (1957), 108.
6. On the subdivision into more than two acts, see Dent, *Mozart's Operas*, 1st edn, 249; 2nd edn, 138 and 168. His general theory may be sound, but the implication that the revision was made in haste in Prague is wrong; there was not enough time, and the preliminary libretto, in any case, is in two acts (see above, n. 5). Act I ends in the middle of the quartet No. 9, but is designed to suggest that this is an act-end, probably so that the censor saw a text with its most licentious scenes omitted (even *Figaro* was

considered by some to be too licentious for a royal honeymoon couple; see Mozart's letter to Jacquin of 15-25 October 1787).

7. Benn, *Mozart on the Stage*, 77ff. He is quite wrong to suggest that da Ponte neglected the time factor. The widely held view of Ottavio as dilatory is quite unjust; he arrives to make an arrest about twenty-four hours after the crime. Ottavio seems indolent because he is usually allowed to sing two elegant arias (properly, they are alternatives). He is still a stronger character than any previous Ottavio, especially Bertati's, who sings an aria of self-pity at the end of the first tableau (where da Ponte has the duet No. 2), and then does nothing except have an inscription carved.

8. That there is a scene-change here is implied by Jahn, *Life of Mozart*, III, 162; therefore by Abert (*Mozart's Don Giovanni*, 44); by Kobbé (*The Complete Opera Book*, 9th edn, ed. Lord Harewood (London, 1976), 106); by Newman (*More Opera Nights*, 341), who says 'Da Ponte requires two settings . . . In Bertati *one* scene suffices'; and by Hughes (*Famous Mozart Operas*, 91). Da Ponte was in fact departing from tradition in having no scene in the country (see p. 40).

9. Moberly, *Three Mozart Operas*, 161 and 184, characteristically taking one possible interpretation of the Italian to imply all sorts of things not intended by da Ponte.

10. Mozart's direction in the score is usually followed; he heads Scene 4 'Notte. Strada'. At bar 23 Leporello says 'essendo cosi tardi' ('as it's getting so late'). But the Prague and Vienna libretti head the scene 'Alba chiara' ('Bright dawn') and Leporello says 'essendo l'alba chiara' ('as it's dawning brightly'). The contradiction is explained by the preliminary libretto, which Mozart probably followed when composing: the scene has no heading, so Mozart supplied one, but it must be 'Notte' since at Elvira's entrance the direction is 'L'alba comincia, e a poco a poco giorno' ('Dawn breaks and becomes day little by little'; Leporello's line is 'essendo verso l'alba', 'as it's getting towards dawn').

11. Hughes points out that famous public figures sometimes have mausoleums erected in their lifetime (*Famous Mozart Operas*, 124).

12. W. Gresser, 'The Meaning of "due della notte" in *Don Giovanni*', *Mozart Jahrbuch* (1971-2), 244. That Mozart knew *Hamlet* is apparent from his criticism of the length of the ghost's speech, but his precept, that such things should be short to be effective, while followed with the *Idomeneo* oracle, was disregarded in *Don Giovanni*, No. 24 (letter to Leopold Mozart, 29 November 1780). Dent refers to the Verona clock (*Mozart's Operas*, 1st edn only, 275-6) and Hughes (*Famous Mozart Operas*, 124) to the Italian six-hour clock; both would indicate 8 or 9 p.m.

13. The additional arias (Nos. 10a, 21b) are given in all scores, but the duet (No. 21a) is omitted or relegated to an appendix. Einstein's Eulenburg score gives it between Nos. 21 and 21b, indicating that the implied sequence is not meant. Unfortunately the edition preceded Einstein's discovery of the authentic recitatives for

Scenes 10b-c; what he published (as Scenes Xc-d) he later deduced to be by a later, not too competent, author for a Prague revival (1801) incorporating the Vienna additions (Einstein, 'Concerning some Recitatives in "Don Giovanni" '). The Neue Mozart Ausgabe alone has all the right recitatives. Its text adheres to the Prague form, placing all Vienna material in the appendix. In Table 2, III was first published by Bitter (1959) *'Don Giovanni* in Wien, 1788'. In IV, the recitative of Ottavio is addressed to Elvira; facsimile of Vienna libretto, Neue Mozart Ausgabe, ed. Plath and Rehm, Vorwort, xiv; in VII and VIII the authentic recitatives were first published by Einstein, 'Concerning some Recitatives in "Don Giovanni" ' (i.e. 1938); in X, some alternative recitative was first published by Bitter, *'Don Giovanni* in Wien, 1788'.

14. Newman, *More Opera Nights*, 379n.
15. Neue Mozart Ausgabe, ed. Plath and Rehm, Vorwort, xiv.
16. Newman, *More Opera Nights*, 345; (cf. Dent, *Mozart's Operas*, 1st edn, 237; 2nd edn, 159).
17. Rank, *The Don Juan Legend*, 38; Jahn, *Life of Mozart*, III, 167; Newman, *More Opera Nights*, 347.
18. Moberly, *Three Mozart Operas*, 161.
19. *Life of Mozart*, III, 167.
20. *Mozart and Beethoven*, 29. Singer's account, which refers directly to Moberly, should (like Moberly's) be read as a whole.
21. Einstein, Eulenburg score, Einführung, xi (repr., xxvii); *Mozart, his Character, his Work*, 439. Moberly (*Three Mozart Operas*, 160 and 167-9) goes so far as to assert that Anna was not only seduced, but enjoyed it. Like Goldoni, he interprets her relationship with Ottavio as one of suppressed hostility. His ingenious fantasy is based on her narration to Ottavio (I. 13), and should be read as a whole; there is no space here to dissect it, for scarcely a line should go unchallenged. It rests on a fallacy, that the narration is equivalent to a musical setting of the scene narrated; thus 'Anna's vocal *grido* (firm but not particularly loud)' is considered to indicate the strength of her scream in her bedchamber. But in telling Ottavio that she screamed, Anna has no need to give a demonstration. Almost equally perverse, and out of step with the musical evidence (see above p. 102), is Mann's view of Anna as a cold person who 'if she loved her father it is because the bible told her so' and for whom 'it would be beneficial to her personal growing up if she had been pleasantly raped by Don Juan' (*The Operas of Mozart*, 468). Pleasant rape is obviously a contradiction in terms; but the real indecency here is to suggest, in line with the worst present-day mores, that she could not care so deeply about her father, nor be horrified by the attempt upon herself.
22. Hoffmann, *Sämtliche Werke*, I, 64. Moberly, following this lead, engages in extravagant vilification of Ottavio, whose chief concern, he claims, is not to get blood on his clothes. At least Hoffmann is only describing a (fictional) performance; Moberly purports to make a critical reading of the text. Again, every line is open to

challenge; for instance, the statement that Ottavio 'took over a hundred bars to dress', an impossible calculation (*Three Mozart Operas*, 173). Apparently Ottavio's critics expect him to run for smelling-salts himself (the servants would know better where to find them) or rush into the dark labyrinth of streets, in hopeless pursuit of the unknown assailant, leaving Anna to come to alone with the body.

23. The source of this chivalrous restraint may be in Molière; Elvire's brother Carlos, under obligation to Juan, will not attack him in his home but is prepared to challenge him in public (V. 3).

24. The direction that Masetto follows at once is often neglected. It puts out of court Moberly's ingenious idea that the 'three orchestra trick' represents not only a device for separating people but 'a deliberate juggling with different time-scales for the purpose of camouflaging the seduction of Zerlina – *before* she screams' (*Three Mozart Operas*, 159). This is odd psychology; Moberly suggests that she screams when she comes to her senses (195), but, in a society which values virginity, sense would dictate silence. Zerlina is not seduced, for she resists; neither, thanks, ironically, to Masetto rather than the masked trio, is she raped. To their credit, producers have obviously begun to look more closely at these directions and include Masetto's swift and effective action.

25. Dent, *Mozart's Operas*, 1st edn only, 273. Hughes concurs, calling the thunder 'purely figurative' (*Famous Mozart Operas*, 110). Abert (*Mozart's Don Giovanni*) included the thunder in his synopsis; curiously enough, this is the only difference between his and Jahn's. On Peter Hall's extravagant response to the thunder, see Higgins, *The Making of an Opera*, 114; it is curious that this should form part of a production which almost uniquely understands the musical implications of the end of the act (not an escape but a static tableau, in 'suspended time').

26. The text translated by Elaine Bleiler, *Don Giovanni*, Dover Opera Guides (New York, 1964), and reproduced in Higgins, *The Making of an Opera*, despite its divergence from Hall's interpretation (on which see p. 97; certainly closer to the letter of da Ponte, if not to his spirit). Jahn, *Life of Mozart*, III, 164; Dent, *Mozart's Operas*, 1st edn only, 273.

27. Moberly, *Three Mozart Operas*, 201, an idea staged by David Pountney (Scottish Opera, 1979).

28. We should not deduce from Leporello's remark in Act II Scene 1, 'Don't think that you can seduce me with money like a woman', that the catalogue is full of professionals. He has of course been so seduced; as for the women, they may have been amateurs less credulous than Elvira or Zerlina, for whom Giovanni needed the seductive influence of gold.

29. These lines are not in the preliminary libretto, although it extends just beyond them to Leporello's next speech ('Più non sperate'). Can the lines have been misattributed?

5 Don Giovanni in the theatre

1. G. B. Shaw, *The Nation*, 22 June 1918, à propos a Carl Rosa performance; repr. in *The Great Composers*, 180.
2. Noske, *The Signifier and the Signified*, 83.
3. The papers did no more than to report the event. Titbits from letters and diaries suggest only that the music seemed out of the ordinary. See Deutsch, *Mozart, a Documentary Biography*, 302ff (Prague, 1787), 314ff (Vienna, 1788); and Mozart's letter to Jacquin of 4 November 1787.
4. Mann (*The Operas of Mozart*, 450) asserts that Mozart must have known Baglioni, but the only 'evidence' is that his sister sang in *La finta semplice* in 1768. Contrary to his usual practice, Mozart does seem to have composed 'Il mio tesoro' for a singer he did not know, before going to Prague. Bitter suggests that a certain pallidity in the role results from this circumstance (*Wandlungen*, 31). On the singers, see *ibid.* 12ff; Procházka, *Mozart in Prag*, 71ff; Abert, *Mozart's Don Giovanni*, 15ff.
5. The silhouettes, the Bassi serenade, and a portrait of Saporiti, are in Bitter, *Wandlungen*, who also has a ground-plan and cross-section of the Prague theatre. See also R. Bory, *The Life and Works of W. A. Mozart in Pictures* (Geneva, 1948), including the cover-picture of the first printed score by Breitkopf und Härtel (1801) and the delightful engravings from the *Almanach Orphea* (1825); and *Mozart und seine Welt in zeitgenössischen Bildern*, Neue Mozart Ausgabe (Kassel, 1961). Bitter prints Bassi's serenade in reverse, because eighteenth-century stage convention demanded that action be directed from right to left. That may be, but would Giovanni play the mandolin left-handed?
6. Bitter's conclusion (*Wandlungen*, 37ff) that the result was an enlightened blend of entertainment and edification may be correct, although it rests partly on the mistaken idea that *dramma giocoso* implies something different from *opera buffa* (see p. 5). The present chapter is, however, heavily indebted to his fascinating study.
7. Deutsch, *Mozart, a Documentary Biography*, 315.
8. On German translations see Jahn, *Life of Mozart*, III, 167; Bitter, *Wandlungen*, 69ff., with a full list in an appendix, 146; Freisauff, *Mozart's Don Juan*, 71-101, particularly on the flaws of Rochlitz; K. H. Oehl, 'Die *Don Giovanni*-Übersetzung von Christian Gottlob Neefe', *Mozart Jahrbuch* (1962-3), 248.
9. Beethoven's strong moral disapproval of certain of Mozart's opera subjects may have begun when he played viola in *Don Giovanni* at Bonn in 1789. His only meeting with Mozart took place during the composition-period of *Don Giovanni*, whose music, of course, he admired.
10. The most authoritative recent lists of performances are those of Bitter (to 1797 only), *Wandlungen*, appendix, p. 145; and Loewenberg, *Annals of Opera*, acknowledging among his sources Freisauff, *Mozart's Don Juan*, and Engel, *Die Don-Juan Sage*.

11. Stiepanek is cited by Nissen, *Biographie W. A. Mozarts*, 522. The hermit episode appears in *Don Juan und Don Pietro oder das Steinerne-Todten-Gastmahl*, a version performed in the eighteenth century at centres including Augsburg, where Mozart had relations. It was also used in plays by Dorimond and de Villiers. (English translation in Mandel, *Theatre of Don Juan*; see Bibliography to Chapter 3.) I am indebted to Edward Forman for this hint; see also Bitter, *Wandlungen*, 76.

12. Deutsch, *Mozart, a Documentary Biography*, 381. Another important early critique is Schink's of the Hamburg *Don Juan*, ibid. 353. Later criticisms are inevitably coloured by Mozart's established reputation, and, in whatever form, *Don Giovanni* was quickly accepted as his grandest, most tragical, even Shakespearian opera.

13. Bitter attributes to Süssmayr in 1798 alterations which the Neue Mozart Ausgabe attributes firmly to Mozart. See Neue Mozart Ausgabe, ed. Plath and Rehm, Vorwort, xiii; Bitter, *Wandlungen*, 61ff and 80, and '*Don Giovanni* in Wien, 1788'. Bitter follows Gugler in this (see below, n. 25), but the indications are generally considered to be in Mozart's hand.

14. The Quaglio sets are sometimes attributed to Joseph (Fig. 1) and Angelo (Fig. 2).

15. On the score, see Einstein, 'Concerning some Recitatives in "Don Giovanni" ', and Köchel, 6th edn, 596. Besides the recitatives it has wind parts omitted from the autograph. On the 1798 Florence attempt see Niemetschek, *Life of Mozart*, 77.

16. Eduard Hanslick, 'Adelina Patti', in *Musikalische Stationen (der Modernen Oper II Theil)* (Berlin, 1885), 24, 26; the article dates from 1879.

17. On Italian performances in the nineteenth century see Petrobelli, 'Don Giovanni in Italia', where every libretto traced is listed.

18. On tempi see Bitter, *Wandlungen*, 32ff and 96ff; W. Gerstenberg, 'Authentische Tempi für Mozart's *Don Giovanni*?', *Mozart Jahrbuch* (1960-1), 58, based on the memories of Jan Vaclav Tomašek.

19. Da Ponte, *Memorie*; P. Nettl, 'Frühe Mozartpflege in Amerika', *Mozart Jahrbuch* (1954-5), 78; R. A. Mooser, 'L'apparition des oeuvres de Mozart en Russie', *Mozart Jahrbuch* (1967), 226 (at 280ff).

20. See D. Arundell, *The Critic at the Opera* (London, 1957), 294ff and 312; A. Loewenberg, 'Some Stray Notes on Mozart. V. *Don Giovanni* in London', *Music and Letters* 24 (1943), 48; W. Ganz, *Berlioz in London* (London 1950), 108.

21. *Wagner Writes from Paris*, ed. R. Jacobs and G. Skelton (London, 1973), 58-63 (quotation (at p. 60) from *Gazette Musicale*, Paris, 18 October 1840); see also p. 120 (*Abendzeitung*, Dresden, 6 April 1841), where Wagner declares that he fell asleep in the Opéra performance.

22. Peacock, *Collected Essays* (1835), cited by J. Barzun, *Pleasures of Music* (London, 1952), 193.

23. Gustave Planche, 'Don Juan à l'Opéra', *Revue des Deux Mondes*,

1834 (I), 667; F. de Langenevais, 'Don Juan', *Revue des Deux Mondes*, 1866 (II), 261, where he shows a rare understanding of Ottavio and Elvira, and *ibid*. 1866 (III), 499, on both Opéra and Théâtre Lyrique performances. Coloured engravings of Nourrit (Giovanni), Cinti-Damoreau (Zerlina), and Levasseur (Leporello), are in *Petite Galerie Dramatique* 9 (Paris, n.d.), nos. 858, 862, 863; these relate to the 1834 production (information from David Charlton).

24. E. Lert, *Mozart auf dem Theater* (Berlin, 1918), 339.
25. F. Chrysander, 'Die Oper *Don Giovanni*'; Freisauff, *Mozart's Don Juan*, Engel, *Die Don-Juan Sage*. Chrysander's *Allgemeine Musikalische Zeitung* had already published several articles by Bernhard Gugler, from 1865 to 1869 (listed by Freisauff, *ibid*. 183), based on a careful study of early sources including the autograph.
26. Maurel, 'A propos de la mise en scène';|see also Petrobelli, 'Don Giovanni in Italia', 42; Shaw, *The World*, 13 May 1891, repr. in *The Great Composers*, 173ff.
27. It is odd that Dent does not mention this staging, if it was this production which he praised for its good sense and unusual intimacy of scale (*Mozart's Operas*, 1st edn, 277). In the Preface to the 2nd edn (ix) Dent dates 'the new outlook on Mozart' from 'Mozart festivals which began in Munich about 1896'.
28. It is necessary to add that while comments on Hall's production are derived as much from Higgins, *The Making of an Opera*, as from the production, those on Pountney's are entirely derived from seeing it in London, and my suggestions about influences upon it (which might include Hall, incidentally, at the end of Act I, where the violence of the storm was combined with the traditional escape) are only inferences.
29. See illustrations of Anna's room with prie-dieu in nineteenth-century French settings; e.g. Chaperon's for the Théâtre Lyrique in 1866 (Bibliothèque de l'Opéra, D. 345, II, 11).
30. Brophy, *Mozart the Dramatist*, 203, and see Chapters XIX and XX, passim.

6 Don Giovanni as an Idea

1. The reader is invited, in preference to suffering the continual interruption of this chapter by footnotes giving precise references, to refer to the works listed in the Select Bibliography by the following: Beauvoir, Berger, Bloch, Camus, Gautier, Hoffmann, Kierkegaard, Massin, Shaw, Stendhal. It is assumed that any consultation of these works would be for the purpose of reading the whole passage. In the passage quoted from Kirkegaard on p. 84 the translation is slightly revised.
2. See Charles Baudelaire, fragment of a scenario, *Le fin de Don Juan*, first published in *Oeuvres posthumes* (1887); Alfred de Musset, dramatic fragment, *La matinée de Don Juan*, first published in *La France littéraire* (1883).

7 The Music

1. Kerman, *Opera as Drama*, 80ff (the trio); Rosen, *The Classical Style*, 296ff (the sextet).
2. I do not accept the musically naive notion that chromaticism in some way represents Giovanni (see Ex. 9, where mourning and vengeance are in the air; that he is the cause of one, and the object of the other, hardly makes chromaticism his motif). Heartz regards the drooping motif of the sextet as a reference to him, but it more obviously amounts to an expression of Elvira's anxious perplexity; its immediate impact is paramount (Heartz, 'Goldoni', 998).
3. This motif E flat – A – B flat ('y' in Ex. 1 without the initial D) is considered as a sort of *Leitmotiv* by Noske: 'Nowhere in the score does the motive appear in the key of B flat without an unequivocal connotation of betrayal' (*The Signifier and the Signified*, 68). The connotation, however, seems remote from Giovanni's mood in 'Fin ch'an dal vino'. Is Mozart supposed to be telling us that Giovanni will betray the girls? Do we need telling? Are we in fact told by the use of so very ordinary a cliché – for does not B flat, like any other key, require the dominant–tonic movement that the notes imply? Although Noske's essay ('Affinities and Structure') is a serious and thorough attempt to grapple with the opera as a musical whole, so many of his connections are so contrived, and the benefits of perceiving them are so very slight, that if anything he enhances a feeling that Mozart's operatic forms are really discrete, and that their unification is as much literary as musical.
4. These lines ('Zitto, zitto, chè la gente Si raduna a noi d'intorno'), Moberly insists, indicate that a crowd is gathering, and this idea was staged by Pountney (see above, p. 76). But to the alarmed Giovanni *gente* can refer to Anna and Ottavio; and the gathering of people on the stage with nothing to do is seldom dramatically successful, and detracts from the cut-and-thrust of Mozart's dialogue. Moberly, *Three Mozart Operas*, 163.
5. *Mozart's Operas*, 1st edn, 236–7.
6. Kerman, *Opera as Drama*, 243, à propos of Ann in *The Rake's Progress*, and Stravinsky's realization of an untapped potential of eighteenth-century opera. Dent, *Mozart's Operas*, 1st edn, 253; 2nd edn, 171. Brophy, *Mozart the Dramatist*, 246. She calls the aria 'Bach-like', a remark of deep perception, the more so since technically her view that Mozart was 'musically archaicizing' cannot be sustained.
7. Berlioz, *Mémoires* (Paris, 1870), Chapter 17. His denunciation of the coloratura (which is very slight by the standards of contemporary *opera seria* or the grand opera of his own day) seems overdone:
   > Donna Anna seems to dry her tears and suddenly delivers herself of indecent buffoonery. . .it is an odd way for the noble, outraged girl to express the *hope that Heaven one day will take pity on her*!. . .I would give some of my blood to wipe out

that shameful page ... one of the most odious and stupid crimes to be found in the history of the art against passion, feeling, good taste, and sense.

Nevertheless, in *Les soirées de l'orchestre* (Paris, 1853), *Don Giovanni* is one of the few operas during which the orchestra does not talk at all.

8. For example Lert, *Mozart auf dem Theater*, 340. Citing Lert, Egon Wellesz calls this passage one of 'dramatic passion' ('"Don Giovanni" and the "dramma giocoso"', *The Music Review* 4 (1943), 124).

9. Kerman, *Opera as Drama*, 121. For Rank (*The Don Juan Legend*, Chapters 2 and 3) and Jouve (*Mozart's Don Juan*, 21), the relationship with Leporello is so intense as to suggest a sort of incest, while Brophy (*Mozart the Dramatist*, 254) rather predictably concludes that Don Juan was a suppressed homosexual (see however above, p. 81 and Chapter 6 passim).

10. D. Tovey, *Essays in Musical Analysis I* (*Symphonies*) (London, 1935), 9.

11. It is instructive to compare this brilliant *coup* with Haydn's key-schemes, for instance in the first finale of *La fedeltà premiata*: B flat – G – G minor – E flat – C – A flat ending E flat – G minor – B flat, and the second, E flat – G – C minor – C – G minor – E flat. The simple reversal of keys seems naive, although Haydn is not a naive composer. Haydn's sections are usually self-contained, Mozart's sometimes run into each other. But above all, the key-shifts of a third in Haydn are used purely for musical effect, and by becoming virtually the norm they altogether lack the dramatic impact of those in Mozart, which first lull us with seductively easy steps down a fifth.

12. On the significance of D, major and minor, see Rosen, *The Classical Style*, 298. M. Chusid considers the evidence warrants associating D minor in Mozart's language with vengeance and the supernatural ('The Significance of D Minor in Mozart's Dramatic Music', *Mozart Jahrbuch* (1965-6), 87). It is difficult to see how all references even to D minor can be construed as having either a structural function or a symbolic value if they are not otherwise related; and the use of a simple motivic idea, at the beginning of the duet proper in No. 2 (Anna: 'Fuggi, crudele'), in the finale (No. 13.3: Elvira: 'Bisogna aver coraggio'), and in the sextet (Anna: 'Lascia alla mia pena'), noted by Rosen and Noske, is as mysterious as the 'quotation' in Ex. 6 above, as even Noske admits (*The Signifier and the Signified*, 52, a laboured attempt to explain Ex. 6, and 54, on the D minor idea: 'the dramatic connotation is far from clear'). The relationship between the Overture, No. 2, and No. 24, is far more cogent, musically and dramatically. Mozart uses few minor keys, so recurrences of D minor are striking more because they are minor than because they are D minor. As for major keys, it is difficult to see how remote recurrences are to be assimilated, except as an analytical game. D major is sometimes said to be Giovanni's key, but this is patently nonsensical, or requires absurdly sophistical explanation,

in (for instance) Nos. 8, 10, 19, and the *scena ultima*. Mozart's range of keys is narrow and each has diverse purposes; F for Leporello (Nos. 1, 24) but for Masetto (No. 6) and Anna (No. 23) as well, and also for seduction (No. 13.2), otherwise carried on in A (Nos. 7, 15).

13. I do not share the common assumption (of Dent, Heartz, Kunze, and Abert) that Mozart 'used' Gazzaniga as da Ponte used Bertati. In both cases the evidence is inferential; in the latter, it is strong. In the former it depends mainly on this Anna–Giovanni scene and the likeness of the violin figure (Ex. 6C, bar 103) and the rhythm, derived from the text. It goes no farther than a few bars (despite Kunze's attempt to draw it over the whole scene; see his edition of Gazzaniga, Vorwort, vii), and the differences are also striking: Gazzaniga has reached the dominant of his first key, E flat, and Mozart goes to the less conventional subdominant of F; Gazzaniga uses a new tempo, Mozart remains at his original tempo. There is no need to defend Mozart since his use of other composers, attested elsewhere, only shows his genius in higher relief; but this case may well be coincidence, given the similarity of the libretti and the unlikelihood of the unpublished Gazzaniga score reaching Vienna in time for Mozart to see it, even if he were interested (whereas a libretto might well travel in a week or two). Other attempts to trace Gazzaniga's influence on Mozart are quite unconvincing; Heartz, for instance, points out Gazzaniga's use of the Neapolitan sixth at the death of the Commendatore and Mozart's extensive use of it throughout *Don Giovanni* ('Goldoni', 997), but Gazzaniga's primitive usage (quoted in Dent, *Mozart's Operas*, 2nd edn, 153) could have taught nothing to the composer of *Idomeneo* or, indeed, *Lucio Silla* (1772; see Act I Scene 7).

14. Noske, *The Signifier and the Signified*, 39. He also (46) makes the point about Leporello's 'D' section anticipating Anna's entrance. On the production problems of this scene see Higgins, *The Making of an Opera*, 83ff, 92, 123, 134; it is obviously the excessive amount of time allowed by Mozart for the action which led to the remarkable idea of having Anna lock Giovanni into the garden!

15. Noske, *The Signifier and the Signified*, 39.

8 The Literature of Don Giovanni

1. Goethe refers to the importance of *Don Giovanni* in a letter to Schiller of 30 December 1797, quoted in Deutsch, *Mozart, a Documentary Biography*, 486; the connection with Faust was made in Eckerman, *Gespräche mit Goethe*, I, 64; see Leo Schrade, *Tragedy in the Art of Music* (Harvard, 1964), 15-16.

2. Complete English translations of Hoffmann's tale are in R. Murray Schafer, *E. T. A. Hoffmann and Music* (Toronto, 1975), 63-73, and J. Barzun, *Pleasures of Music* (London, 1952), 29-40.

3. Mozart's saying that he wrote *Don Giovanni* 'Not at all for Vienna, to some extent for Prague, but mostly for myself and my friends'

relates to his well-attested preference for this opera; it is uncertain what was Berlioz's source.

4. Schumann, 'Ein Opus 2', *Gesammelte Schriften*, 5th edn (Leipzig, 1914), I, 5 (repr. from *Allgemeine Musikalische Zeitung*, 1831).

5. The titles of episodes in *Ulysses* are taken from Stuart Gilbert, *James Joyce's Ulysses* (London, 1930); page references are to the Penguin edition of *Ulysses* (Harmondsworth, 1968).

Select bibliography

Don Juan plays, libretti, scenarios, and anthologies thereof are separately listed; see below, Bibliography to Chapter 3.

Abert, A. A. *Die Opern Mozarts.* Wolfenbüttel and Zurich, 1970–
    Chapter I (d): 'The Operas of Mozart', *The Age of the Enlightenment,* ed. F. W. Sternfeld and E. Wellesz (New Oxford History of Music, VII). London, 1973
Abert H. *Mozart's Don Giovanni* (extracted and trans. by P. Gellhorn from *W. A. Mozart* (Wiesbaden, 1924), Abert's revised 6th edn of Jahn, *Life of Mozart;* some of this book is, in fact, by Jahn, but is not so attributed) London, 1976
Abraham, G. 'The Operas', *The Mozart Companion,* ed. Landon and Mitchell, 283-323, esp. 296-301 and 320-1
Anderson, E., ed. *The Letters of Mozart and his Family.* 3 vols. London, 1938
Angermüller, R. and Schneider, O. *Mozart-Bibliographie – Mozart Jahrbuch,* 1975
Austen, J. *The Story of Don Juan: a Study of the Legend and of the Hero.* London, 1939
Beauvoir, S. de. *Pour une morale de l'ambiguité.* Chapter 2, 22ff. Paris, 1961. Trans. B. Frechtman, *The Ethics of Ambiguity.* New York, 1967
Benn, C. *Mozart on the Stage.* London, 1946
Berger, J. *G.* London, 1972
Berlioz, H. *Les musiciens et la musique.* Paris, 1903
Bitter, C. *Wandlungen in den Inszenierungsformen des 'Don Giovanni' von 1787 bis 1928: zur Problematik des Musikalischen Theaters in Deutschland* (Forschungsbeiträge zur Musikwissenschaft, X). Regensburg, 1961
    'Don Giovanni in Wien, 1788', *Mozart Jahrbuch* (1959), 146-64
Bloch, E. *Das Prinzip Hoffnung.* 'Don Giovanni, alle Frauen und die Hochzeit', Part 5, section 49, 92ff. Berlin, 1953–6
Brophy B. *Mozart the Dramatist.* London, 1964
Bucher, A. *Mozart and Prague.* Prague, 1962 (illustrations; see also Chapter 5, n. 5)
Camus, A. *Le mythe de Sisyphe.* 'Le Don-Juanisme', 97–105. Paris, 1942
Chrysander, F. 'Die Oper *Don Giovanni* von Gazzaniga und von Mozart', *Vierteljahrszeitschrift für Musikwissenschaft* 4 (1888), 351-435
Clarke, R. *Don Juan. Studies in Dramatic Characterization.* Sheffield, 1961

154   *Select bibliography*

Clive, G. 'The Demonic in Mozart', *Music and Letters* 37 (1956), 1–13

Croxall, T. H. 'Kierkegaard on Music', *Proceedings of the Royal Musical Association* 73 (1946–7), 1–11

Dallapiccola, L. 'Notes on the Statue Scene in "Don Giovanni" ', *Music Survey* 3 (1950), 89-97

Dent, E. J. *Mozart's Operas. A Critical Study*. London, 1913; 2nd edn, London, 1947

Deutsch, O. E. *Mozart: Briefe und Aufzeichnungen*. 7 vols. Neue Mozart Ausgabe. Kassel, 1962–75

Mozart, a Documentary Biography. London, 1965

Diet, E. *Regards sur l'Opéra*. 'Don Juan et Chronos: note psychoanalytique sur le final du Don Giovanni de Mozart', 241–57. Rouen, 1976

Einstein, A. *Mozart, his Character, his Work*. London, 1946

Essays on Music. 'The First Libretto of "Don Giovanni" ', 217-20. London, 1958

'Concerning some Recitatives in "Don Giovanni" ', *Music and Letters* 19 (1938), 417-25 (also *Essays on Music*, 221-31)

(ed.) Mozart, *Don Giovanni* (Eulenburg miniature score 918). London, n.d. (*c.* 1930), Foreword in German; repr. London, n.d. (*c.* 1960) with Foreword also in English

Engel, K. *Die Don-Juan Sage auf der Bühne*. Dresden, 1887

Fitzlyon, A. *The Libertine Librettist: a Biography of . . . Lorenzo da Ponte*. London, 1955

Freisauff, R. von. *Mozart's Don Juan*. Salzburg, 1887

Gautier, T. *Histoire de l'art dramatique en France depuis 25 ans.* 'Italiens: Don Giovanni' [1845], IV, 35ff. Paris, 1858–9

Gendarme de Bévotte, G. *La légende de Don Juan*. Paris, 1911

(see also Bibliography to Chapter 3, Anthologies)

Gounod, C. *Le Don Juan de Mozart*. 3rd edn. Paris, 1890.

Grau, J. See Bibliography to Chapter 3, Anthologies

Heartz, D. 'Goldoni, Don Giovanni and the dramma giocoso', *The Musical Times* 120 (1979), 993–8.

Higgins, J. *The Making of an Opera: Don Giovanni at Glyndebourne*. London, 1978

Hoffmann, E. T. A. *Sämtliche Werke*, I. 'Don Juan', 62-73. Munich and Leipzig, 1912

Hughes, S. *Famous Mozart Operas*. London, 1957

Jahn, O. *The Life of Mozart*. 3 vols. (trans. P. Townsend from *W. A. Mozart*, 2nd edn, Leipzig, 1867). London, 1882 and 1891

Jouve, P.-J. *Le Don Juan de Mozart*. Paris, 1942. Trans. E. E. Smith, *Mozart's Don Juan*. London, 1957

Kerman, J. *Opera as Drama*. Chapters 3 and 4: 'Action and the Musical Continuity' and 'Mozart', 73–128. New York, 1956; London, 1957

Kierkegaard, S. *Either/Or*, I (trans. D. F. and L. M. Swenson). 'The Immediate Stages of the Erotic', 37-110; see also 'Diary of the Seducer', 249–371. Princeton, 1944. (original edn 1843)

Köchel, Ludwig von *Chronologisch-thematisches Verzeichnis sämtlicher*

Tonwerke Wolfgang Amadé Mozarts. 6th edn, ed. F. Giegling, A. Weinmann, and G. Sievers. Wiesbaden, 1964

Kunze, S. *Don Giovanni vor Mozart. Die Tradition der Don-Giovanni-Opern im italienischen Buffa-Theater des 18 Jahrhunderts*. Munich, 1972

'Mozarts *Don Giovanni* und die Tanzszene im ersten Finale', *Analecta Musicologica* 18 (1978), 166-97

(ed.) G. Gazzaniga, *Don Giovanni*. Kassel, 1974

Landon, H. C. R., and Mitchell, D., ed. *The Mozart Companion*. London, 1956

Lert, E. *Mozart auf dem Theater*. Berlin, 1918

Lesure, F., ed. Mozart, *Don Giovanni* (facsimile of the autograph score). Paris, 1967

Liebner, J. *Mozart on the Stage*. London, 1972

'Don Juan et ses ançêtres, ou la métamorphose d'une légende', *Schweizerische Musikzeitung* 104 (1964), 237–43

Livermore, A. 'The Origins of Don Juan', *Music and Letters* 44 (1963), 257-65.

Loewenberg, A. *Annals of Opera, 1597-1940*. Cambridge, 1943

Lorenz, A. 'Das Finale in Mozarts Meisteropern', *Die Musik* 19 (1926–7), 621–32

Lorenzi de Bradi, M. *Don Juan. La légende et l'histoire*. Paris, 1930

Macchia, G. See Bibliography to Chapter 3, Anthologies

Mandel, O. See Bibliography to Chapter 3, Anthologies

Mann, W. *The Operas of Mozart*. London, 1977

Marchesan, A. *Della vita e delle opere di Lorenzo da Ponte*. Treviso, 1900

Massin, J. See Bibliography to Chapter 3, Anthologies

Maurel, V. *A propos de la mise en scène de Don Juan. Réflexions et souvenirs*. Paris, 1896

Moberly, R. B. *Three Mozart Operas*. London, 1967

Mozart, W. A. *Il dissoluto punito o sia Il Don Giovanni*, editions: see Einstein; Lesure; Plath and Rehm
Letters: see Anderson: Deutsch

Müller, F. W. 'Zur Genealogie von Leporellos Liste', *Beiträge zur Romanischen Philologie* 9 (Berlin, 1970), 199–228

Nettl, P. *Mozart in Böhmen*. Prague, 1938 (revision of Procházka, *Mozart in Prag*)

'Die Spanische Seele des Don Giovanni', *Mozart Jahrbuch* (1959), 262–5

Newman, E. *More Opera Nights*. London, 1954

Niemetschek, F. X. *Life of Mozart* (trans. by H. Mautner, of *Lebenbeschreibung des K. K. Kapellmeisters Wolfgang Gottlieb Mozart*, Prague, 1798). London, 1956

Nissen, G. N. *Biographie W. A. Mozarts*. Leipzig, 1828

Noske, F. *The Signifier and the Signified. Studies in the Operas of Mozart and Verdi*. Chapters 3 and 4: '*Don Giovanni*: Musical Affinites and Dramatic Structure', and '*Don Giovanni*: An Interpretation', 39-92. The Hague, 1977.

Obliques 4 and 5 (n.d.). *Don Juan* issues (4 with full bibliography)

Petrobelli, P. 'Don Giovanni in Italia', *Analecta Musicologica* 18 (1978) (colloquium 'Mozart und Italien'), 30—51

Plath, W. and Rehm, W., ed. Mozart, *Don Giovanni*. Neue Mozart Ausgabe II/5/17. Kassel, 1968

Ponte, L. da *Il dissoluto punito o sia Il Don Giovanni, dramma giocoso in due atti* [libretti] (1) Vienna, 1887 [preliminary libretto] ; (2) Prague, 1887; (3) Vienna, 1888. See also Plath and Rehm (critical edn of score)

    Memorie. New York, 1823—7; 2nd edn, 1829—30. Trans. as *Memoirs of Lorenzo da Ponte* by L. A. Sheppard, London, 1929, and by E. Abbott, Philadelphia, 1929

Procházka, R. *Mozart in Prag*. Prague, 1892

Rank, O. *The Don Juan Legend* (trans. and ed. D. G. Winter from *Die Don Juan-Gestalt*, Leipzig, 1924). Princeton, 1975

Rosen, C. *The Classical Style: Haydn, Mozart, Beethoven*. London, 1971

Rousset, J. *Le mythe de Don Juan*. Paris, 1978

Shaw, G. B. *Man and Superman. A Comedy and a Philosophy*. London, 1903

    Short Stories, Scraps and Shavings. 'Don Giovanni Explains' (1887). London, 1934

    The Great Composers, Reviews and Bombardments, ed. L. Crompton (from various sources). Berkeley and Los Angeles, 1978

Singer, I. *Mozart and Beethoven: the Concept of Love in their Operas*. Chapter 2: 'The Conflict in Don Giovanni', 24-73. Baltimore, 1977.

Smith P. J. *The Tenth Muse: A Historical Study of the Opera Libretto*. Chapter 11: 'The fin-de-siècle Italian Libretto', 161-79. London, 1971.

Stendhal (Beyle, M. H.) *De l'amour* (1822). Chapter 59: 'Werther et Don Juan', 230ff. Paris, 1959

Table Ronde, La, 119 (November 1957). *Don Juan* issue

Tan, H. G. *La matière de Don Juan*. Leyde, 1976

Tiersot, J. *Don Juan de Mozart*. Paris, 1933

Weinstein, L. *Metamorphoses of Don Juan*. Stanford, 1959

Werner-Jensen, K. *Studien zur 'Don Giovanni' — Rezeption in 19. Jahrhundert*. Tutzing, 1980

Bibliography for chapter 3

Don Juan before da Ponte (Texts)

Anthologies

Gendarme de Bévotte, G. *Le festin de pierre avant Molière*. Paris, 1907 (texts: Dorimond, de Villiers, Biancolelli)

Grau, J. *Don Juan en el drama*. Buenos Aires, 1944 (texts: Tirso, Molière, Goldoni, some later versions)

Macchia, G. *Vita, avventure e morte di Don Giovanni*. Bari, 1966 (texts: *L'ateista fulminato*, Biancolelli, *commedia dell'arte* scenario (Rome, Biblioteca Casanatense), Cicognini, *L'empio Punito*)

Mandel, O. *The Theatre of Don Juan*. Lincoln, Nebraska, 1963 (texts, in English, with commentary: Tirso, Molière (trans. J. Ozell, 1714), Shadwell, da Ponte, later versions)

Massin, J. *Don Juan, mythe littéraire et musical*. Paris, 1979 (texts, with commentary: Tirso, Molière, Hoffmann, Pushkin, Lenau, Baudelaire (in French), da Ponte (in French and Italian))

Spaziani, M. *Don Giovanni dagli scenari dell'arte alla 'Foire'*. Rome, 1978 (introduction and texts: Le Tellier (*forain*), two *commedia dell'arte* scenarios (Naples, Biblioteca Nazionale, and Rome, Biblioteca Casanatense), *L'ateista fulminato*, Biancolelli)

Individual texts

Bertati, G. *Don Giovanni o sia Il convitato di pietra*. Limited edn, on sale at performances. Siena, 1973
    See also Select Bibliography, Chrysander; Kunze (critical edn of score)

Goldoni, C. *Don Giovanni Tenorio*. Ed. G. Ortolani (Goldoni, *Opere*, IX). Rome, 1950

Molière, J. B. *Don Juan ou le festin de pierre*. Ed. W. D. Howarth. Oxford, 1958 (full discussion of sources with synopses). In English: J. Wood, *Molière: The Miser and Other Plays*, Harmondsworth, 1968; G. Graveley, *Six Prose Comedies of Molière*, London, 1968

Tirso de Molina (pseudonyn of G. Téllez). *El burlador de Sevilla y Convidado de piedra*. Ed. A. Castro. Madrid, 1922 (repr. 1975). Ed. G. E. Wade. New York, 1969. Bacquero, A., *Don Juan y son evolucion dramatica* I. Madrid, 1966 (*El burlador* and *¡Tan largo* *me lo fiáis!*). Trans. Roy Campbell in E. Bentley, *The Classic Theatre*, III. New York, 1959; A. Flores, *Masterpieces of the Spanish Golden Age*, New York, 1957

Discography

MALCOLM WALKER

G Giovanni   Normal version   Overture, Nos. 1–10, 10a, 11–
A Anna   21, 21b, 22-4 (see p. 5)
E Elvira   Prague version   Overture, Nos. 1–24
O Ottavio   Ⓜ mono recording
L Leporello   ④ cassette version
M Masetto   Ⓔ electronically reprocessed stereo
Z Zerlina   all recordings are in stereo unless otherwise stated
C Commendatore

1936 Brownlee G; Souez A; Helletsgrüber E; Von Pataky O; Baccaloni
L; Henderson M; Mildmay Z; Franklin C/1936 Glyndebourne
Festival Chorus and Orch/Busch
Normal version   Turnabout Ⓜ THS65084–6

1942 (live performance – Metropolitan, New York) Pinza G; Bampton
A; Novotna E; Kullmann O; Cordon L; Harrell M; Sayão Z;
Kipnis C/Metropolitan Opera Chorus and Orch/Walter
Normal version   Cetra Ⓜ LO27/3

1943 (in German) Ahlersmayer G; Schech A; Teschemacher E; Hopf
O; Böhme L; Frick M; Weidlich Z; Pflanzl C/Dresden State
Opera Chorus, Saxon State Orch/Elmendorff
Normal version   DG Ⓜ LPEM19250-2

1950 (live performance – Salzburg Festival) Gobbi G; Welitsch A;
Schwarzkopf E; Dermota O; Kunz L; Poell M; Seefried Z;
Greindl C/Vienna State Opera Chorus, VPO/Furtwängler
Normal version   Olympic Ⓜ 9109/4
                              Turnabout THS65154-6

1950 Stabile G; Grob-Prandl A; H. Konetzni E; Handt O; Pernerstorfer
L; Poell M; Heusser M; Czerwenka C/Vienna State Opera Chorus,
Vienna SO/Swarowsky
Prague version; appendix, Nos. 10, 21b
                              Nixa Ⓜ HLP2030/1–4
                              Haydn Society Ⓜ HSLP2030/1–4

1951 (broadcast performance – N. German Radio, Hamburg) Schöffler
G; Martinis A; Danco E; Dermota O; Kunz L; Neidlinger M;
Hoffmann Z; Hofmann C/North German Radio Chorus and
Orch/Ludwig
Version unknown   Melodram Ⓜ MEL015

1953   Taddei *G*; Curtis Verna *A*; Gavazzi *E*; Valletti *O*; Tajo *L*; Susca
       M; Ribetti *Z*; Zerbini *C*/Turin Radio Chorus and Orch/Rudolf
       Normal version   Cetra ⓔ LPS3253
                                 Everest-Cetra ⓔ 403/3
1954   (live performance – Salzburg Festival) Siepi *G*; Grümmer *A*;
       Schwarzkopf *E*; Dermota *O*; Edelmann *L*; Berry *M*; Berger *Z*;
       Ernster *C*/Vienna State Opera Chorus, VPO/Furtwängler
       Normal version   Cetra ⓜ LO7/4
1955   Siepi *G*; Danco *A*; Della Casa *E*; Dermota *O*; Corena *L*; Berry
       M; Gueden *Z*; Böhme *C*/Vienna State Opera Chorus, VPO/Krips
       Normal version   Decca GOS604–6
                                 London OSA1401
1955   London *G*; Zadek *A*; Jurinac *E*; Simoneau *O*; Berry *L*; Waechter
       M; Sciutti *Z*; Weber *C*/Vienna State Opera Chorus, Vienna SO/
       Moralt
       Normal version   Philips ⓜ GL 6768 – 033
                                 Philips/Mercury ⓔ PHC–3–009
1956   Campo *G*; Stich-Randall *A*; Danco *E*; Gedda *O*; Cortis *L*; Ves-
       sières *M*; Moffo *Z*; Arié *C*/ Aix-en-Provence Festival Chorus,
       Paris Conservatoire Orch/Rosbaud
       Normal version   Pathé ⓜ DTX218–21
                                 Vox ⓜ OPBX1623
1956   (live performance – Salzburg Festival) Siepi *G*; Grümmer *A*;
       Della Casa *E*; Simoneau *O*; Corena *L*; Berry *M*; Streich *Z*; Frick
       C/Vienna State Opera Chorus, VPO/Mitropoulos
       Version unknown   Replica ⓜ RPL2422–5
1958   Fischer-Dieskau *G*; Jurinac *A*; Stader *E*; Haefliger *O*; Köhn *L*;
       Sardi *M*; Seefried *Z*; Kreppel *C*/Berlin Radio Chorus and SO/
       Fricsay
       Normal version   DG 2728 003
1958   Colombo *G*; Kingdom *A*; Graf *E*; Giraudeau *O*; Ollendorf *L*;
       Gorin *M*; Dobbs *Z*; Hofmann *C*/Netherlands State Opera Chorus
       and Orch/Krannhals
       Version unknown   Concert Hall SMS2121
1959   Siepi *G*; Nilsson *A*; L. Price *E*; Valletti *O*; Corena *L*; Blankenburg
       M; Ratti *Z*; Van Mill *C*/Vienna State Opera Chorus, VPO/
       Leinsdorf
       Normal version but with No. 21a included between Nos. 21 and
       21b   Decca D10D4
                                 RCA (US) LSC6410
1959   Waechter *G*; Sutherland *A*; Schwarzkopf *E*; Alva *O*; Taddei
       L; Cappuccilli *M*; Sciutti *Z*; Frick *C*/Philharmonia Chorus and
       Orch/Giulini
       Normal version   HMV SLS5083 ④ TC–SLS5083
                                 Angel SDL3605
1965   Ghiaurov *G*; Watson *A*; Ludwig *E*; Gedda *O*; Berry *L*; Montarsolo
       M; Freni *Z*; Crass *C*/New Philharmonia Chorus and Orch/
       Klemperer
       Normal version   HMV SLS923
                                 Angel SDL3700

1966 Fischer-Dieskau *G*; Nilsson *A*; Arroyo *E*; Schreier *O*; Flagello *L*; Mariotti *M*; Grist *Z*; Talvela *C*/Prague National Theatre Chorus and Orch/Böhm
Normal version   DG 2711 006 ④ 3371 014

1969 Bacquier *G*; Sutherland *A*; Lorengar *E*; Krenn *O*; Gramm *L*; Monreale *M*; Horne *Z*; Grant *C*/Ambrosian Opera Chorus, ECO/Bonynge
Normal version but with No. 21a included between Nos. 21 and 21b   Decca SET412-5
London OSA1434

1973 Soyer *G*; Sgourda *A*; Harper *E*; Alva *O*; Evans *L*; Rinaldi *M*; Donath *Z*; Lagger *C*/Scottish Opera Chorus, ECO/Barenboim
Prague version, with Nos. 10, 21a, 21b in appendix, plus some recitative to No. 21a   HMV SLS978
Angel SDL3811

1973 Wixell *G*; Arroyo *A*; Te Kanawa *E*; Burrows *O*; Ganzarolli *L*; Van Allan *M*; Freni *Z*; Roni *C*/Royal Opera Chorus and Orch/C. Davis
Normal version   Philips 6707 022 ④ 7699 054

1977 (live performance – Salzburg Festival) Milnes *G*; Tomova-Sintov *A*; Zylis-Gara *E*; Schreier *O*; Berry *L*; Düsing *M*; Mathis *Z*; Macurdy *C*/Vienna State Opera Chorus, Salzburg Mozarteum Orch, VPO/Böhm
Normal version   DG 2790 194 ④ 3371 042
DG(US) 2709 085 ④ 3371 042

1978 Raimondi *G*; Moser *A*; Te Kanawa *E*; Riegel *O*; Van Dam *L*; King *M*; Berganza *Z*; Macurdy *C*/Paris Opera Chorus and Orch/Maazel
Normal version   CBS 79321 ④ 40-79321

1978 Weikl *G*; M. Price *A*; Sass *E*; Burrows *O*; Bacquier *L*; Sramek *M*; Popp *Z*; Moll *C*/London Opera Chorus, LPO/Solti
Normal version but with No. 21a included between Nos. 21 and 21b   Decca D162D4 ④ K162 K4
Londa OSA1444

1979 (in German) Grundheber *G*; Koszut *A*; Gomez *E*; Harder *O*; Ahrens *L*; Nielsen *M*; Bracht *Z*; Hölle *C*/Ludwigsberg Festival Chorus and Orch/Gönnenwein
Normal version   EMI 1C 155 99810-3

Index